PETER ANDRE
THE BIOGRAPHY

PETER ANDRE

THE BIOGRAPHY

LOUISE FORD

JOHN BLAKE

Published by John Blake Publishing Ltd,
3 Bramber Court, 2 Bramber Road,
London W14 9PB, England

www.johnblakepublishing.co.uk

www.facebook.com/Johnblakepub facebook
twitter.com/johnblakepub twitter

First published in paperback in 2013

ISBN: 978-1-78219-443-9

British Library Cataloguing-in-Publication Data:

A catalogue record for this book is available from the British Library.

Design by www.envydesign.co.uk

Printed in Great Britain by CPI Group (UK) Ltd

1 3 5 7 9 10 8 6 4 2

Papers used by John Blake Publishing are natural, recyclable products
made from wood grown in sustainable forests. The manufacturing processes
conform to the environmental regulations of the country of origin.

Every attempt has been made to contact the relevant
copyright-holders, but some were unobtainable. We would be
grateful if the appropriate people could contact us.

CONTENTS

CHAPTER ONE
ANGELS AND DEMONS

Peter Andre stares at the camera and flashes one of his winning smiles. Sat in the back of a blacked-out car, he is the vision of showbiz cool: his hair spiked with forensic precision and designer suit immaculately pressed, nothing is out of place.

Minutes later, he's joined by his beautiful children, Junior and Princess, who climb onto the seat behind him. Nestled between them is his stunning student girlfriend, Emily MacDonagh, who chuckles affectionately at the youngsters' jokes.

It's a heart-warming scene entirely in keeping with the singer's public image that every second is a photo opportunity – a snapshot that wouldn't look out of place on the pages of the glossy magazines he's adorned so many times before.

Except this is real life. His eyes sparkle with genuine happiness. And true to form, the perfectly composed pin-up soon crumbles into Peter Andre, the down-to-earth dad-of-two the public has come to adore. As seven-year-old Junior and Princess, five – the family he had with glamour girl Katie Price during their infamous four-year marriage – start discussing with excruciating honesty his new and blossoming love life, Peter curls with embarrassment.

Begging them to stop talking with Emily just inches away, Princess tells him in a way only a five-year-old could: 'You do love my Mum but you love Emily more.' 'Yes, yes, yes, you love Emily more,' his son pipes up, grinning at the red-faced couple. And as defeated Peter drops his head in his hands and groans: 'Oh dear Lord, I'm going to have a heart attack!', angelic-looking Junior pulls out his trump card and announces triumphantly: 'My Dad doesn't want to marry my mum, only Emily!'

From the mortified look on Peter's face it's clearly something he hadn't planned to discuss just a few months into his fledgling relationship, much less on camera in front of the 1.3 million fans who have tuned in to watch the latest ITV2 series of *Peter Andre – My Life.*

Medical student Emily – who was a family friend for two years before they started dating and is referred to by Princess as her 'best friend' – collapses into a fit of giggles.

Life is clearly good for Peter and it's unlikely just three years previously he could have imagined himself at the centre of such a happy scene.

In 2009 he walked out on his marriage to reality TV star Katie Price after a tumultuous six years and two children together. While she reverted to partying and dating a series of men before marrying cross-dressing cage fighter Alex

Reid a year later, Peter spoke only of his distress at their divorce and his desire to protect their family, including Katie's eldest son, mentally and physically disabled Harvey.

'I believe marriage is for life and this has left me utterly devastated,' he said at the time.

It was clear both of them were knocked for six by their split but were dealing with it in very different ways. But for Peter, with over 20 years in show business it was obvious overcoming hard times had become second nature to him.

It would be fair to say even to this day that for every positive twist in Peter's 40 years of life – the first record deal, the emergence of 'Peter Andre' the nineties pop star, the fairytale wedding to Katie Price and his romance with Emily, an intelligent trainee doctor 16 years his junior – there was seemingly a turn for the worse...

The failed marriage, his very public divorce, the impending court cases, rows over custody of his children and latterly the loss of his beloved eldest brother Andrew to cancer.

And that was just what he was famous for. His seemingly unrelenting 'glass half full' attitude also hid a multitude of dark secrets behind closed doors.

It's a little known fact, Peter James Andrea – as he was born – was raised a Jehovah's Witness in a tough suburb of London and while his parents worked tirelessly to provide a loving home, his childhood was strict, orderly and sometimes frightening.

When the Greek Cypriot family moved to Australia when Peter was six, he was racially abused, later threatened by gangs and as a pop star in his 20s even endured terrifying death threats. By the time he reached adulthood and at the height of his fame Peter had become a master of concealment as he performed to thousands of fans while suffering crippling panic attacks which became so bad he was admitted to a psychiatric hospital.

But throughout all the good, the bad and every twist and turn, there have been two constants in his life which he has continually drawn strength from: music and his close-knit family.

From an early age writing music and performing became his form of therapy and a way of escaping from the pressures life kept throwing at him. His family, meanwhile, has always been the glue that held him together and helped propel Peter to become the star, and now father, he always dreamed of being.

In 2012, his toughest year yet and five months before Andrew lost his nine-month battle with kidney cancer, Peter admitted he was never going to let life's difficulties get the better of him.

'The last year has been all about fighting for me. Fighting to give myself and my kids a future, fighting all my fears, fighting for my brother...' he told the *Sun* newspaper.

And whatever his future held, the twice-crowned Dad Of The Year was adamant that along with his family, he would face every challenge head-on. 'Family is No. 1 to me and I was definitely brought up to believe that. Of course I do worry about my children and my family, but with everything else in life, I just think whatever happens, happens.'

In Peter's case, despite his gleaming smile and infectious

laugh, a surprising amount has happened in his 40 years of life.

And if we go right back to the beginning – and to pinch the name of his latest 2012 album – there seem to have been a fair amount of angels and demons along the way.

CHAPTER TWO
GROWING PAINS

M any have come to regard Peter Andre as the perfect portrait of a family man. His children, he has admitted many times over, are his life and every important decision is made with them at the forefront of his mind. Even while going through one of the toughest divorces in showbiz history to Katie Price, critics were stunned at Pete's ability to remain tight-lipped to protect those dearest to him. While the former Page 3 girl dealt with the split by clubbing and dating a string of new men, those closest to the couple knew that Pete's only way of survival was to stay close to his roots and look to his family for support.

So it's no surprise that his favourite childhood memory still remains one of his family – mum, dad and five siblings – coming together every night for dinner at their modest home in Harrow, Northwest London.

True to their Greek heritage, it was simply a chance for the children and their parents Savva, a barber and his seamstress wife Thea – to switch the TV off, sit down at the table and enjoy a good old-fashioned hearty meal while chatting about the day's events.

Peter, the youngest of five boys – Andrew, Chris, Danny, Michael and a girl, Debbie – remembers: 'Every dinner time we would all sit together at the dining-room table. After Mum had served up food, Dad would always say a prayer before we were even allowed to pick up our knives and forks. I remember Chris would kick my leg to try to make me laugh.

'Because Dad's prayer was always in Greek we couldn't understand half of what he was saying anyway. But it was always the same routine.

'We were cheeky little kids and just couldn't wait to eat. I just remember thinking, "Well, he's only got three more breaths to go."'

At first glance, you may be forgiven for thinking Peter James Andrea – born on 27 February 1973 at London's Northwick Park Hospital – had something of an idyllic childhood.

His father Savva moved to England when he was 20, speaking no English but determined to learn a trade. As one of 12 children growing up in Cyprus he wanted a large family of his own and London in the early 1950s seemed to have all the opportunities on which to build his dreams.

After the Second World War ended in 1945, Britain's capital was at the centre of a massive economic boom. As with many other cities, London had suffered severe damage in the war after being bombed extensively by the Luftwaffe during The Blitz and needed to be rebuilt. Immigrant workers from all over the world, including Europe and the Caribbean, started to arrive in their droves to help build millions of new homes and help boost industry.

Peter's parents were right at the centre of a golden age when jobs were plentiful, businesses were starting to flourish and houses, including high-rise flats and streets of new build family homes, were springing up everywhere to accommodate the expanding population. Savva managed to get a job as a barber and a year after meeting Thea – a hardworking young dressmaker – in 1954, the pair married.

Peter's mum, a woman who he once described as 'pure love', always remained true to her Greek roots and was devoted to doing everything in her power to make her husband and children's life happy. She too was an industrious woman with drive and ambition, and in the early years worked out of her own shop.

Although they were hardly well off, Savva eventually managed to save up enough money to buy a store three doors down from Thea's business in London's Paddington and his dreams of a mini empire of his own started to come to fruition. By the time Peter was born, nearly 20 years later his father had done exceptionally well for himself. Along with a barber's shop upstairs, he ran a women's hair salon below and owned an incredible 17 houses in Notting Hill and Barons Court. Savva and Thea continued to work hard to make sure they never went without and although the family was now reasonably wealthy and money wasn't tight, Peter was adamant they were never spoilt.

'Back then everything was done in cash and my parents had so much they didn't know where to put it!' he recalled. 'But I wasn't born with a silver spoon in my mouth – my father always told me I had to work hard.'

Peter spent the first six years of his life at 1 Sudbury Court Road, Harrow – a typical 1970s family home. As well as Paisley wallpaper, thick pile carpets and a 100-foot garden with apple trees, the six siblings shared two bedrooms between them.

With his parents both born into large Greek families, there was no question they wanted the same for themselves but even so, Pete had long been convinced that with 16 years between himself and his eldest brother, Andrew, he had been a mistake.

'I know that after Mum and Dad had had two boys, they really wanted a girl,' he said. 'But they kept getting more boys until they had my sister and they were content... then I came along!'

Whether his suspicions were correct or not, the Andrea house was filled with a lot of love. The road the family lived on felt 'protected and friendly' too, with a multi-cultural mix of Pakistani, Jamaican, Italian, Spanish and Jewish neighbours all living happily side by side. Idyllic days were spent playing with local children in the street outside their home, hunting for conkers on nearby Sudbury Hill and Peter remembers taking Greek dishes to their Pakistani neighbours for dinner, while they would bring curry round to theirs.

At six years old, Pete had three important people in his life outside of his family: his best friend Jamie Roberts, his favourite teacher Mrs Bye at Sudbury Junior School and his first girlfriend, a Sri Lankan girl called Miranda Madurasinghe.

'I used to carry her satchel like a true gent!' he remembered later, 'It was the real thing alright. We used to hold hands under the desk and at six years old that feels like the most amazing thing. I remember INXS brought out a song called "Original Sin" which referred to the dream of love between a white boy and a black girl – that was how it was with me and Miranda. We were in love.'

To the outsider, it certainly looked like the picture-perfect childhood but in truth it was far from conventional. His parents – in particular, his father – were strict Jehovah's Witnesses and insisted the family follow the teachings of the Bible in all aspects of their lives. Pete was terrified of his dad, which was mostly due to Savva's fearsome reaction to his son's bad school reports and the fact that he was constantly getting into fights with his classmates. In the Andrea household bad behaviour meant the children were severely reprimanded and beaten.

'At home I was always scared of Dad, although it was my three elder brothers who got the worst of it, as he disciplined them quite hard,' he later recalled. 'They would often get a wallop but that was no different to any other families. What I was really scared of was Dad's voice, which used to make me shake.'

Peter even admits, to this day, that he is still afraid when his father speaks to him in a certain tone, even though after heart-to-hearts in recent years he has apologised to his son for not being more affectionate when he was little. Having said that, Peter has plenty of fond memories of times they shared together.

As a very young boy, Peter used to enjoy sitting in the passenger seat of his dad's seemingly huge Mercedes, a car that even then signified success, as the businessman visited his various friends and associates around London. Peter also savoured the times when his father sent him on errands to Ted's sandwich bar, round the corner from his parents' shops in Paddington to buy him a ham sandwich for lunch. Ted's wife, clearly enamoured with such a tiny, angelic-looking customer – and much to his father's delight – often gave him the sandwiches for free.

But despite being the doted upon and much-loved youngest child of the Andrea brood and in a house filled with all the usual noise and chaos typical of any large family, Peter often felt frightened and alone at night, something he's keen his own children, Junior and Princess, will never have to experience.

'My parents were very strict,' he remembers. 'I had to go to bed really early and I was always lonely – it's not my parents' fault – but I just felt very scared and lonely at night.' He added, speaking to parenting website, Parent Dish: 'Now I've put little things in my kids' rooms, like these little glowing universes and I tell them that the angels are watching over them.'

But at school, the future pop star put on a far braver front and much to his parents' dismay was often getting into fights with other pupils. Although he was never the kid who started trouble, he was the class 'show-off', which meant he wanted to be the hero in defending those pupils being picked on by bullies. Teachers often found Peter right at the centre of a punch-up.

It didn't just happen once or twice but before long being summoned to see the headmaster, Mr Harris, was a common theme to Peter's early years at primary school. Inside the head's office, and at a time when corporal punishment was still legal, Peter was often caned or given a 'plimsoll pudding' – an affectionate term at the time for being hit with a shoe. As a consequence his attention in the classroom started to slide and his school reports were bad, which in turn landed him in trouble at home.

'Whenever it was school report time I'd run up to my room when Dad came home as I was never a high achiever,' Pete remembers. 'I'd pray to God that Mum had received my report because she couldn't understand English!'

At one point the school, in desperation at not being able to correct his wayward attitude, sent Peter to a psychologist. It was around this time that life was taking a turn for the worse for the whole family. For starters they were no longer living on the 'friendly little street' which Savva and Thea had chosen to raise their children. One day, Peter's older brother Chris came home with his hands covered in blood. He had been stabbed in a fight with his best friend.

It was a horrifying incident that happened during a time when the capital was changing. The late seventies saw mass unemployment and a wave of strikes in London, while IRA bombings brought fear to its streets. Violent gangs also started to emerge across the city, with racism and poverty rife. Even on Peter's tree-lined residential street in North-

13

west London, the neighbours were more likely these days to be peering out from behind closed curtains than talking over the garden fence.

The final crunch came when two gangs on motorbikes roared into the street and started fighting with chains. Enough was enough for Peter's parents and they decided to bring their family up in safety, near the sea and in the sunshine. In 1979 they held a family meeting and announced they were moving to Australia.

'They just sat us down one day and said, "Get packed because we're going to Australia!" The truth slowly started to sink in. Mum cried a lot; I don't think she wanted to go. I know Dad did, though, because while half his family had moved to Britain, the other half had moved out there,' Peter remembered.

It was a turning point in his life and one that changed it forever. Not just because he was forced to say goodbye to good friends and the only life he'd ever known but somehow the move to the other side of the world cemented his passion for music, something he would one day look back on with fond memories.

Even as a six-year-old in that suburban street in Harrow, Peter was already a fan of Motown. As a schoolboy he would spend hours in his shared bedroom listening to the records his older brothers brought home, including Al Green, James Ingram and Luther Vandross.

But he was also an avid listener of the radio, too. The 1970s was becoming a golden age for soul and reggae music in multi-cultural London and Peter was terrified stations in Australia wouldn't be playing the music he had grown to love. So frightened was he of never hearing his favourite songs again that he recorded his top 10 tracks from the radio onto a cassette tape and packed it in his bags. As it turned out, he played that tape over and over again during some very difficult settling-in years in Australia to remind him of 'home' – a feeling he still claims he didn't experience again until he returned to Britain, 20 years later.

Life in Australia wasn't all bad – far from it, though. In many ways it was the making of him. The family arrived in Sydney for a fresh start and everyone seemed happy. Far from feeling like strangers, Savva was able to introduce his wife and children to long-lost aunts, uncles and cousins they had never seen before. But after a holiday to the Gold Coast in Queensland, Pete's parents decided to up sticks again in 1982 and move to a town called Surfers Paradise, with its promise of crystal-white beaches and family-friendly outdoor living. Sadly, not only was it 600 miles away from the hustle and bustle and noise and pollution of Sydney, it was also worlds apart from the capital's affable and multi-ethnic community that Pete had grown to love.

In Queensland, the schoolboy and his family stood out. It was always going to be tough for a black-haired, brown-eyed kid with an English accent to fit in. The town had seen few 'foreigners' before, particularly Greeks and Italians, and much to the family's horror, they were called 'wogs' – a derogatory term against black people they had previously heard back in London.

'We ended up in a part of the world where we least fitted in,' Andre told the *Mail On Sunday*. 'We were this bunch of dark-haired, dark-eyed, Greek Jehovah's Witnesses living in the middle of blue-eyed, blond-haired surfer dudes. The only constant thing in my life was music. I was obsessed by Michael Jackson and George Benson but even that made me stick out because all the kids at school were into surfer music and rock. I guess I was an outcast from the start.'

For the first time in his life, instead of being the hero standing up to the bullies, Peter was the one being bullied, with no one to fight his corner. It began within three days of starting his new primary school and lasted for many years, making his school years 'gut-wrenchingly miserable'. Peter was consistently picked on and many times found himself tied to a fence while children threw stones at his head and beat him up. Even the teachers berated him for having a different accent and he spent much of his time feeling completely isolated from the other pupils.

'There was so much racism and I realised I was the complete underdog because I was ethnically different. Even though I'd get the shit beaten out of me by the other kids, I was always too proud to cry and I never snitched,' he recalls, years later. His classmates remember a similar story. 'I'd say he would have hated his school life because he was a skinny little shit. We used to play basketball before and after school, as well as lunchtime, and he would try and join in but he was hopeless,' said one. 'He was the wimp who always got picked on.'

The long-term consequences of being so berated for his appearance was as soon as Peter was wealthy enough to take action, he had plastic surgery on his nose. He told the *Daily Mail*: 'I had my nose done because there was a little hook on it that I really didn't like and the kids used to tease me about it at school.'

Coupled with the abuse, it was this less-than-perfect perception that got Peter interested in body building and working out. He was 13 when he first decided, against his father's wishes, to start martial arts lessons: he wanted to learn how to protect himself and send a message to the bullies that he could fight back. It proved something of a turning point. After becoming proficient in a range of disciplines including kickboxing and Kung Fu, Peter found immediately that it had the desired effect.

'I'm a very anti-violent person but there was one occasion when I was forced to use my kickboxing skills to defend myself. There was this guy from my kickboxing class who was annoyed because he wanted to be the best and he didn't like me being so good at it. He hit me so hard one night walking home that I lost my temper and ended up giving him a real hiding. I've never given anyone a beating like that. I had taken so much of it when I was younger that I was not going to take it now; I knew how to look after myself. From then on people knew that I was no longer the kid to be picked on,' he told the *People* newspaper in 1996.

While the family suffered tough times both at school and in the community, far from breaking them, it served to bring the Andrea clan closer together. Living on the Gold Coast beneath the hot Australian sun meant weekends fishing at the Great Barrier Reef with their father, barbecues in the back garden and Pete's favourite, sand-surfing along the beach.

But while their childhood was idyllic in many respects, it remained markedly different from other local kids' upbringings, with Peter's parents raising them as Jehovah's Witnesses. Savva and Thea had converted from Greek Orthodox after a persuasive doorstep encounter at their London home in the late sixties. For Peter and his siblings it meant following the key rules, as set out in the Bible: respect your elders, clean living and no adultery. The children would have to attend Watchtower classes on Sundays, book study on Tuesdays and Theocratic Ministry meetings on Thursdays. It also meant Peter was forbidden from celebrating Christmas Day and birthdays as they are regarded by the religion as pagan festivals.

Peter celebrated his first ever Christmas Day at the age of 31 in 2004 with his then new girlfriend, Katie Price and her eldest son, Harvey. To many the thought of being a child and never having experienced waking up on Christmas Day to see if Santa had been, or blowing out candles on a birthday cake seems remarkably cruel but Pete has always maintained he didn't mind going without. Nor did he care about the times when he was in Bible meetings when he knew his friends would be out playing together.

'I was never jealous,' he insisted. 'Christmas was only ever a hard time for us when we were living in England and that was because it was always cold and snowing outside. When you don't expect something you don't get disappointed.

'When kids at school boasted about the gifts they'd been

given I used to think about everything we had as a family. I always tried to think of the positive things and that's a trait I inherited from my father.

'My parents were always very fair. They never let us go without. Mum and Dad always taught us that you don't have to wait until a special occasion to give someone a gift. I follow the same principal today.'

The religion also taught him good manners and most significantly for Peter the importance of a strong bond with family. He even joined his parents door-to-door where they tried to convert people to the religion when he was 15.

'I never actually felt that comfortable about it,' he remembers. 'My grandfather did three-mile walks every day, witnessing door-to-door, until he was 93 years old. I never rebelled against it. My greatest fear was to become an apostate (one who deserts the faith), but that didn't happen.'

When Peter was 17 he started to question his faith and realised that he had a decision to make: either he believed or didn't believe, he couldn't sit on the fence anymore.
'So I simply stopped practising,' he told the *Mail On Sunday*. 'There was no family row. No bad feeling. The other aspect of my family is the very traditional Greek side. We love each other – we'd die for each other. My parents and my family have always been, and remain, the most important people in my life.'

For his parents though, their greatest fear was for their teenage son's passion for singing and the prospect that if he succeeded in his ambition of getting into the music industry it would lead to an unsavoury life of sex, drugs and rock'n'roll.

'I used to tell them how George Benson was an Elder in the church and he had a career. But they were petrified,' he said.

While Peter remains defiant that his religious upbringing and teachings always kept him away from drugs, they didn't stop him from indulging in music – and as we will discover, numerous women.

An interview with Peter at the height of his early fame in 1996 summed it up. 'Rock'n'roll? I'm not into that. And as for drugs, forget it. But sex? Let me be a sinner... let me be a sinner!' he told the *Sunday Mail*.

In fact, it was his faith that had given him his first taste for music. It was at church meetings in Wembley that Peter discovered he enjoyed singing and it quickly became an important part of his life.

'I used to sit there and hear people singing hymns and that gospel stuff and I'd think, "Wow, one day I'd just love to get up like those gospel singers did and have that aura on stage! That was my dream at school and I don't think I ever dreamed of anything else,' he said in an interview with *Smash Hits* magazine in the early 1990s.

It was in Australia, though that his passion for music really started to ignite and he began putting his plan for a pop career into action. Being so lonely at school Peter transformed his bedroom into a haven of everything he missed from back 'home' in England. The walls were covered in posters of Michael Jackson, Bob Marley, Stevie Wonder and Elvis, and he would stand in front of them and lose himself in singing their songs. He remembers belting out hits for so long sometimes that his throat would hurt.

As well as the 10-track tape he had brought with him from London, the wannabe pop star, who continued to refuse to tune into Australian radio, started to buy albums. His first was Michael Jackson's *Off The Wall* in vinyl and listening to it transported him back to Sudbury Court Road in Harrow. That started Peter's obsession with the King of Pop. Not only did he love his music, but he identified with the young Michael's feelings of isolation from other children.

He remembers reading how the American star was six or seven years old rehearsing inside a studio and wondering why he wasn't like the other 'normal' children having fun in the playground outside.

'I used to do the same,' Peter recalls, 'I used to look out of the window and think, "Why aren't I like those kids in the park?" I always felt like an outsider – always!'

So important was Jackson's influence in his life that he told ITV News shortly after the rock star's untimely death in 2009 that he was 'devastated', adding: 'Michael was my biggest influence, musically and in a lot of ways. He made me dream of being on stage, he made me dream of wanting to be part of music, plus they were a very inspirational, loving family.'

Like Jackson, Peter wanted to one day be accepted by all those who had treated him as an outsider. He knew he couldn't change his personality or the colour of his skin but he was convinced that becoming a singer would make him happy.

Focusing on his sole ambition of being famous enough to have the cash to fly back to England and appear on

BBC's *Top of the Pops*, the schoolboy managed to persuade his parents to transform the garage into a rehearsal space. His devoted father, clearly realising his son's genuine passion for music and wanting to nurture it, bought him some speakers. Peter promised to pay him back a dollar a week but Savva refused to take it.

His brother Chris also remembers how his younger sibling was always showing off and wanting to try out his latest dance moves in front of the whole family. 'We'd all be sitting in front of the TV and Peter would burst into the living room and he just started dancing and carrying on,' he recalls affectionately.

Chris, who was very musical himself, also recognised his brother's talent and they started writing songs together. One of them – called 'Dream A Little' – went on to appear on Peter's first album. Then at 13 years old, he had a major breakthrough when he was given the opportunity to sing in public for the very first time. Luckily for him the lead singer of the band in the annual school concert had fallen ill and his music teacher, Mrs Challenger, agreed to let Peter have a go. Shaking with nerves, Pete managed to stand in front of a thousand people in the school hall and perform his own version of Stevie Wonder's 'I Just Called To Say I Love You'.

The reaction was phenomenal and after giant applause from the audience his teacher turned to him and said what he'd always wanted to believe: 'You've got something, go for it!'

Peter, now at his new senior school Benowa High, found the performance did wonders for his reputation and he started to hang out with the 'cool kids', known as the Rat Pack. His best friend George Nicolau was also a Greek-Cypriot from Canberra, who had faced similar bullying and racist taunts growing up in Australia, so the duo instantly had a sense of camaraderie.

They also hung out with a red-haired aspiring actor called Craig Ball and the best-looking guy in the school, Christian Fry, who thanks to his popularity with the girls meant the whole group started getting a lot of attention.

As well as growing into a handsome young man, the young teen also had a new identity in the sense that he was now known as Peter Andre, with the final 'a' dropped off. His brother Mike, who was a few years older and popular in school, had become so incensed with his schoolmates trying to pronounce the silent 'a' when saying his surname that everyone knew not to try it on with Peter.

It was around that time that Pete, who as a skinny 13-year-old had taken up martial arts in a bid to stand up against the bullies, followed his older brothers Michael, Danny and Chris in working out at the gym at their local youth centre. Guided by his siblings, Peter started building himself up into the 10-stone power-pack he would became famous for a decade later, by lifting weights and hitting punch-bags. He became hooked and a few years later his skinny frame had started to develop into the firm, muscular body millions of women lusted over in the nineties.

'I had abs to die for,' he wrote later. 'At school all I could think about was the lunch break, when I could nip into the gym and work out.'

But it was starting to turn into a dangerous obsession.

There was the added temptation back at home where his older sister Debbie, like many teenage girls, had started to get into dieting and was putting herself on low-calorie eating plans. Peter was fascinated by it and started joining her in turning down their mum's hearty meals of lamb chops and chips in favour of fruit and protein shakes. As well as doing three or four sessions a week in the gym of kickboxing, punches and sit-ups, he would go for a run along the beach every morning after breakfast. His new look meant girls were also starting to notice him.

By the time he was 16, toned and full of testosterone, Peter and his Rat Pack friends were going to nightclubs three times a week to drink, dance and try and meet women. Having older brothers meant many of the bouncers at the door knew who he was and they let him through to the bar, where they knocked back beer and the drink du jour: Southern Comfort and Coke.

But something for Peter didn't feel right. It was difficult to continue leading such a hedonistic lifestyle while still being a practising Jehovah's Witness at home. He had been taught by his Elders there was nothing worse in God's eyes than sitting on the fence and being a hypocrite. One minute he was going to meetings, the next he was bending the rules left, right and centre, so he could continue having fun. Peter stopped attending meetings but out of respect for his parents, he made sure they neither witnessed him drunk nor learned of his misadventures.

Not long afterwards, at 17 years old he lost his virginity with a girl from his drama class. Blonde-haired Melanie

Cooper was in the year below and after starting out as good friends, they quickly became an item. The chemistry between the pair was undeniable but inexperienced Peter for a long while was too scared to take it much further than kissing. But one night back at her beachside apartment listening to their favourite Anita Baker album, they finally had sex.

'Poor Melanie! We were teenagers when that happened. I tried to act cool but at that time it was over pretty quick because I was so young,' Peter told Piers Morgan on his ITV series *Life Stories* in 2011.

After that first disastrous night of passion Peter was determined to hone his skills in the bedroom – with a little bit of advice from his older brothers.

'My brother Danny used to call me "Mr Minute" when I was younger, because there was this place in Australia where you could get your keys cut in a minute so I started training my mind to last for a minute and then it went on for ages!' he added.

Peter and Melanie remained an item for another 18 months until, much to his distress, she moved to New Zealand with her parents. After that it wasn't just his interest in women that was growing stronger but his dreams of pop stardom were intensifying, too. With backing tracks recorded onto a cassette tape and a catalogue of songs he'd learned off by heart, Peter started to enter talent contests in local pubs and bars.

'I was obsessed with being a pop star and I entered every talent contest going,' he told the *Daily Mirror* in 1995, 'But you can bet your last dollar I lost every one of them.

'I couldn't even win a competition on the back of a cornflakes packet!'

Peter's persistence paid off, though and spurred on by school friends who had finally started to see his talent, he applied to star on Australia's most popular TV talent show, *New Faces*. In a format very similar to *Britain's Got Talent*, wannabe singers and performers were scored by a panel of judges, with the winners going on to greater success in the TV and music industry.

Having got through the tough audition stage in his hometown of Queensland, Peter was one of seven hopefuls – including three other singers, a juggler, comedian and a dancer – to get through to the final in 1990. Waiting in the wings of the Channel 9 studio for the show to start, he was terrified. Outside was the studio audience, two million viewers at home and a team of judges including record producer Ian 'Molly' Meldrum – the Simon Cowell of his generation, who had the power to make or break an artist in minutes.

Dressed in an all-black outfit, save for a black and white polka-dot waistcoat borrowed from one of his brothers and white socks in the style of his all-time hero, Michael Jackson, Pete was finally waved onto stage. Despite his crippling nerves and ridiculous outfit, he managed to belt out a pitch-perfect rendition of Bobby Brown's classic 'Don't Be Cruel' and pull off a dance routine choreographed by his brother's friend Victor to perfection.

'You are a natural, a star,' the first judge told him, to the studio audience's rapturous applause. The second judge, a choreographer, said he would have liked more versatility in his moves before adding, 'but as for star quality, you've definitely got it.'

The most important critique was yet to come and Pete wasn't disappointed.

'I wouldn't mind you coming to talk with me. I own Melodian Records and I think you're it! You're going to be a huge star,' Molly told him.

It was the first time in Australian history that an artist was given a record deal live on air.

That night Peter enjoyed all the spoils of being the winner of a TV show and experienced his first taste of the high life when the production company put him up in a luxury hotel with chocolates and champagne in his room. But the next day the elated teenager came back down to earth with a bump when he had to return home, go back to school and wait for the call from Molly Meldrum's record company. There was no word for six long months.

'I said to my Mum and Dad, "Maybe it's not going to happen, maybe it's all just been a dream." I started to become depressed,' he remembered later.

'I couldn't face going to school, where people would pester me with "Have you heard?" and I'd have to tell them, "No, not yet."'

Finally he got a call from the director of Mushroom Records (a branch of Melodian), who flew to his home in Surfers Paradise to give him the contract he'd been so desperate for. His dreams were finally becoming a reality but it was hardly a story of overnight success. In fact it took an astonishing two years since his appearance on *New Faces* to release his first single.

CHAPTER THREE
TOP OF
THE POPS

Peter's first foray into the music charts flopped spectacularly. He finally released his first single, 'Drive Me Crazy', with Mushroom Records in 1992 which, despite promises from the label of nurturing his career until the moment was right, struggled to reach No. 72.

Thankfully it was quickly followed by a second release, 'Gimme Little Sign', which was an instant success. It was the ticket to fame that Peter had always craved and the nineties idol with the ultra-chiselled torso and cheesy chart-topping hits was starting to emerge. By the end of the decade he had notched up 15 Top 50 singles in both the Australian and UK charts as well as three albums, including his 1996 chart-topper *Natural*, which went platinum in Britain.

But it was a decade of contradictions for Peter: as well as the elevated highs of Top 10 records, wild affairs and world tours with some of the biggest artists in history, there were unbelievable lows, including death threats, gay rumours, lost loves and eating problems. This eventually led to a breakdown and what seemed like the end of his career for good.

'It was all there: the world tours, the success in Europe, the women, the sex, the unbelievable amount of sex, and then it ended,' he admitted later.

But at the start of his fledgling career it all seemed to be going so well. The single 'Gimme Little Sign' was so successful in Australia – where the label initially focused Peter's career – it stayed in the ARIA charts (Australia's official music chart) for a staggering three weeks, reached No. 3 and was the sixth biggest single of the decade.

You would never have known from the grin on his face and happy-go-lucky interviews while promoting it on endless TV and radio shows that the pin-up boy with his greased-back, floppy hair wasn't happy with it.

'"Gimme Little Sign" was my ticket to stardom but I hated it,' he admitted some years later. 'To me it was too cheesy. And cheesy was to haunt me for years.' Regardless of what he thought, the public loved it.

And although he might not have loved the tune itself what Peter did like about producing the single was that it had proved that the key ingredient in turning a decent pop song into a chart-topping sensation was his body. 'I knew my physique attracted the girls so I thought why not show it off while I'm performing? The only guy that I'd seen who was doing this was American star Mark Wahlberg or "Marky Mark" as he was known and people were going crazy for his music as well as his ripped, sexy look.'

So before its release and against advice from the record company who were adamant it wouldn't work, Peter carefully repackaged his look to appeal to his female fans, taking a mix of Michael Jackson's dance moves and fashion style and honing his muscular body like Hollywood actor Jean-Claude Van Damme.

His suspicions were spot-on. Having his rippling abs on display seemed to be as important to his growing army of fans as the catchiness of his songs. It was no wonder that for years after Peter became increasingly obsessed with maintaining his body and image in a bid to keep selling records.

'The six-pack stomach was a marketing ploy,' he told the *News Of The World* in 1996, 'the old saying sex sells is true.'

More singles followed, with 'Funky Junky' and 'Let's Get It On/Do You Want To Dance?' making the Top 20, along with his first album in 2003 entitled simply *Peter Andre*.

It was clear that he was fast becoming a major star with a bright future ahead of him. His face was splashed across covers of teenage magazines, newspapers were falling over each other to get interviews and he was appearing on some of the country's biggest TV chat shows. But being in the public eye, Peter was quickly discovering, wasn't all glitz and glamour; it came with a very dark side. Many people didn't want a squeaky-clean celebrity in their midst – they wanted scandal.

It wasn't long before the press and music industry became rife with rumours Peter was gay. When he and his then manager Molly Meldrum appeared together on the

TV show *Good Morning Australia* in 1992 to promote the track 'Gimme Little Sign' rumours they were secret lovers were already circulating.

'Despite his name I didn't know Molly was gay and famous for signing young boy bands, especially "good looking" ones.

'Throughout the industry and especially in the music press whispers were going round that I must be gay too, they thought I was Molly's toyboy. I may have a pretty face but I was only interested in girls,' he wrote later.

False reports about his sexuality persisted for many years and weren't helped by Peter appearing naked in a magazine when he was 19, on Molly's insistence. Although he was allowed to preserve his modesty in the pages of trendy pop publication *Black and White* his deeply religious parents, Savva and Thea, were devastated.

'To be honest, Molly never made advances towards me but I always felt uncomfortable and I started to resent homosexuals for the tag that was being put on me,' he said.

Little did everyone know – from journalists to agents to his legions of female fans – that, not only was Peter not gay, he wasn't young, free and single either. Kathy Maddock, a stunning Australian dancer, was dating the emerging pin-up but with his record company eager not to disappoint his now thousands of adoring fans, the pair were forced to keep their romance strictly under wraps.

While his new music video for 'Gimme Little Sign' was being broadcast across Australia, with Peter oozing sex appeal dancing between two beautiful women in skimpy bikinis on Bondi Beach, Kathy was ordered to stay out of the limelight at all costs. It was something Peter felt guilty about for many years afterwards but with his team threatening: 'You mention her and your career's not going to happen,' he felt there was no choice.

And with his music going from strength to strength, the next big stage in his career – going on tour across Australia supporting top American artist Bobby Brown – was a dream come true.

Peter had been hauled into Mushroom Records head office by top boss Michael Gudinski, who promoted some of the world's biggest artists in Australia, including Madonna, Elton John and the late Michael Hutchence, to be told the good news. Convinced he was going to get a dressing down from Gudinski for something he'd done wrong, he was overwhelmed to discover he was being handed his own 90-minute set at the start of Bobby's show, with his brother Chris on guitar as his own support act.

Bizarrely, the tour's opening night was three years to the day since Peter had appeared on *New Faces* and won with one of Bobby Brown's songs.

'I got a real kick out of that. Back then Bobby was the coolest guy you could imagine, like 50 Cent or Jay-Z nowadays. Just to meet him was a dream come true. For the kid who'd been the odd one out at school it finally felt like I'd been accepted,' he remembered in his autobiography, *Peter Andre: My World*.

Much to his amazement even Bobby himself, one of his all-time greatest idols who was married to none other than Whitney Houston, seemed to accept him too. As they toured the full length of Australia together he was quickly welcomed into the millionaire singer's inner circle, one filled with all the debauchery and trappings of fame.

For young and impressionable Peter being privy to Bobby's taste for wild all-night parties and flings with young fans, as well as witnessing people taking Class A drugs right in front of him for the first time was a huge eye opener. It was starting to become clear that the deeper he was getting into a more successful and glittering career, the more out-of-control his own life was becoming. The strong moral code he'd been taught by his parents was quickly disintegrating as he struggled to maintain this new image of 'Peter Andre the star'.

While to this day he claims to have resisted every temptation to take drugs despite cocaine 'being handed round like candy', women were fast becoming his weakness. For the first time in his life – and going against everything he believed in – he cheated on Kathy with one of the dancers in Bobby's entourage. The fling didn't last long after she slept with another man behind his back at one of the tour's cocaine-fuelled parties and in a move Peter wasn't proud of, he kept up the pretence nothing had happened and continued playing the faithful boyfriend to his lover back home.

Kathy, who only realised Peter's infidelities after four years together, got her revenge many years later when she appeared on the 2004 TV documentary *Mysterious Man* about his life and career by saying: 'Peter wasn't a great lover. In bed he was concerned in case I touched some area that wasn't toned in the way he wanted it to be. He was built small, I've had bigger.'

But staying faithful to a woman thousands of miles away

had at that point become impossible for 18-year-old Peter. He was finding his popularity with female fans was one of the few positive aspects of increasing fame. Life on the road was intimidating and lonely, having only lived with his parents before, and he was struggling to eat and drink. Not only that, the death threats had started.

One of the worst came before one of Bobby's shows when Peter received a letter with a chilling message made from words cut out of a newspaper. It read: 'When the colour turns blue, watch the light and watch who's watching you. Death awaits'. Peter knew there was a section in his performance of 'Gimme Little Sign' when he would appear under a blue spotlight.

Police officers who had been called in to investigate were worried that due to a series of violent clashes in Sydney between Greek, Italian and Lebanese gangs there was a very real danger to Peter's life and a strong possibility that he could be shot onstage in front of thousands of fans. They told him it was too risky to perform and advised him to stand down. Peter refused and in one of the most frightening hours of his life managed to get through the set surrounded by 26 police officers to protect him.

Having survived the tour in more ways than one, he returned home, where life regained some stability, and he released his first album, *Peter Andre* – a record he was really proud of. Musically, Peter was doing incredibly well; the record peaked at No. 27, his singles were being played endlessly on Australian radio and 'Funky Junky' was regularly used as a theme tune on hit TV soap *Neighbours*. Girls were throwing themselves at him and he was getting fan mail by the sackload but even his sex appeal was attracting some unwanted attention. An obsessed blonde fan discovered where he lived and began stalking him.

'I used to talk to her. I thought she was sweet. But then she started turning up to my shows, claiming she was my fiancée and that she was pregnant with my child,' he remembered.

One night he looked out of his window at 3am and saw her standing on the kerb.

'No one knew where I lived – except her. She also knew my phone number. So we stepped up security. The last thing she sent me was a photograph of herself looking down a barrel of a gun. Very creepy. I think the gun meant the end of her obsession, she was going to stop, not that she was going to kill herself,' he told the *Daily Mirror* in 1996.

Thankfully for Peter 'the show had to go on' and next came a six-week stadium tour supporting Madonna on the Australian leg of her *Girlie* tour.

Now known as 'The Body' to his fans, Peter admitted the Queen of Pop was everything he'd imagined her to be – 'a confident and sexy lady' – and still being reasonably new to the industry, he was intimidated by her world-wide fame.

'I fell over backwards when I heard I was to be Madonna's support. I was trying to pluck up the guts to talk to her but she came over to say thanks for doing the show and asked if I was being treated well. She was really genuine,' he told the *Sunday Mail*.

Unlike the wild and often illegal backstage antics of Bobby

Brown's tour, Peter found that he and Madonna shared an obsessive pre-show health and fitness regime instead.

'When I did shows with Madonna she was jogging five miles a day but for me doing sit-ups was my way of getting ready. At that point I was doing 300 sit-ups before a show. I was ripped before going on,' he said on Australia's *Not The Jack Docherty Show* in 1997.

The shows were a sell-out success and when Peter was performing in front of 80,000 people some nights, the applause when he came off stage was deafening. But for every high, there was a low, and one evening when he left one of the venues people started hurling abuse at his car. It was something that was starting to become a regular occurrence and each night Peter didn't know what to expect – cheering fans or being abused and spat on. He had begun to realise that while for many he was a likeable pop idol, for others he was fast becoming a figure of hate.

'There was no other young kid having this kind of success in Australia at that time and it was obvious there were as many people out there who took against me as there were fans. Maybe some of the guys were jealous of the attention I was getting from women.

'Perhaps it was that, but I think it was simply that a lot of people didn't like me,' he admitted.

From then on the threats started to escalate and the situation went from bad to worse. Just as he was preparing for his own arena tour, Peter was at the centre of a terrifying ordeal in Sydney when an armed gang threatened to kill him. The star was walking through the city's red-light district when 12 men jumped him and pulling out knives and chains, told him they would 'slice' him up.

Thankfully they were all talk and no action but Peter couldn't work out their motives nor what he could do to stop it. He wasn't even safe back home on the Gold Coast where he'd grown up either. Letters sent through his post box threatened to kill his family with terrifying messages like 'I hope your mum and dad are going to sleep well tonight because we're keeping a close eye. Tell them not to sleep too deeply'. He was also getting racist-fuelled death threats from Middle Eastern gangs and knives pulled on him at nightclubs where he'd once gone to escape and have fun.

Peter now had to hire security guards for protection because nowhere felt safe anymore. Not only that, people everywhere seemed to be poking fun at the way he looked – his long hair, his clothes. Where he had once been the golden boy of pop he now felt like a national joke.

'I hated my life. I hated Australia and I hated the record industry for doing this to me,' he said.

His ticket to sanity came when the record company agreed to send him to England to write another album. It was time to leave Australia, along with his girlfriend Kathy, who he promised to return to one day 'soon' to marry her.

In December 1994, a few days after the Madonna tour, he flew to London with the firm determination to crack his lifelong ambition of headlining Wembley Arena and appearing on *Top of the Pops*.

'I went from not being able to walk down the street without minders to nobody really knowing me or recognising me.

'In a way it was quite nice but I was young and ambitious and I wanted to make it big over here too, nothing was going to stop me.'

Peter had recorded a few tracks for his new album in a London studio when he started begging Mushroom Records to let him release a single in the UK. The record company – which worked from a tiny office on London's King's Road – resisted, saying they didn't think he would appeal to a British market which was rock-heavy at the time with artists like Sheryl Crow, Jon Bon Jovi and Green Day in the Top 10. But the star believed he had something unique to bring to the music scene – he was a single male artist with both a catalogue of solid pop songs and a body for fans to lust over. While it had worked for American artists like Mark Wahlberg and heartthrob rapper Vanilla Ice, there was no solo UK artist attempting to do the same and with a niche in the market, Peter was desperate to spread his profile.

Refusing to take 'no' for an answer he begged the label to let him do some Under-18 shows at youth clubs across the UK. They eventually agreed – but the conditions said it all. The fee would be £10 a night, Peter would be provided with a small Peugeot to drive himself to the gigs and he was to buy his own petrol. It was laughable compared to the showbiz lifestyle with all the minders, chauffeurs and entourage he'd left behind in Australia but he didn't care – he was just thankful for the opportunity to prove them wrong. The first gig, with a set list that included a mix of his hits from Australia and the songs he'd recorded for his new album, went down a storm.

He was turning up at concerts with no one knowing who he was, but by the end being mobbed out the door by teenagers begging for more.

'The response was wild. Even at my peak in Australia it had never been like this. I didn't know what hysteria was until I came to England,' he admitted.

Peter knew he was on to something and started building a fan club by handing out cards which said: 'If you want more information about Peter Andre write to this address...' Soon enough, Mushroom Records' modest UK headquarters were flooded with letters from fans, not just in their thousands, but tens of thousands. The record company had promised once there were 20,000 names and addresses on their database it would consider releasing a single and with this target now achieved and doubling, it wasn't long before Peter was given the green light to make a new record.

His first British release 'Turn It Up', in June 1995, despite the massive fan base limped into the charts at No. 64. Undeterred and psyched by the reaction at his live gigs Peter signed up to do the *Mizz* magazine road show, the must-have tour for all up-and-coming artists. And it was at a gig on the Isle of Wight when he met the woman who was to change his career forever, Claire Powell – then co-owner of Blitz Management, which had a second-to-none reputation in the music industry for discovering and developing new talent.

When he came off stage, straight-talking Claire told him: 'I've been speaking to Mushroom Records and I'm interested in managing you.

'I see the potential – you have to let me manage you.'

Without agreeing to anything, Peter rang his dad back home for advice. He asked him if he should ditch Molly Meldrum in Australia, the man who had given him his first break, for this new British manager, who seemed to think that under her guidance he could break the UK once and for all. Knowing his son's contract in Australia was up for renewal and after looking at the paperwork Peter had faxed through from Blitz Management, Savva agreed that making the switch was the way forward.

It was the approval Peter was looking for and plucking up all his courage he called Molly, who to his amazement wasn't angry but seemed happy to let him go and wished him luck.

From that point on, Peter seemed to climb higher and higher up the pop ladder.

With his fan base growing by 4,000 a week Claire proposed to Mushroom Records that he should start touring schools across Britain to tap further into the teen market.

'Mushroom weren't that keen on investing in me but Claire is a mighty persuasive lady who doesn't take no for an answer. Thank God she doesn't, that tour made me,' he remembered, years later.

Peter was fast becoming a runaway success at every school assembly, where he would perform a few of his hits and then do a question-and-answer session about his experience in the music industry and his anti-drug stance. This was often followed by local radio and press interviews and sometimes an Under-18 gig in the evening.

His work schedule was now so gruelling he was only getting four or five hours' sleep a night and life on the road meant staying in seedy, often dirty hotels and eating in roadside cafes. It was undeniable the plan was working, though; whenever Pete left a gig hundreds of girls would mob him in the car park and the hysteria was reaching such a level he hired his brother Danny to be his security guard.

Riding on the crest of a wave and with the school tours almost exhausted, Claire's next step was to get in touch with some old friends of Peter's who he'd met in Australia: a London band called East 17, who had said they would love to tour with him if he was ever in the UK.

Band member Brian Harvey remembered the Australian hunk instantly and made sure he was included in the line-up for their sold-out 1995 European tour. Even though Peter had to pay for the privilege, Claire thought it was worth it. The chart-topping rap band, which included frontman Tony Mortimer, were at the height of their fame with two albums under their belt and a string of Top 10 hits including 'House Of Love', 'Deep' and No. 1 hit, 'Stay Another Day'.

'East 17 had huge street cred at the time, they were a bit like N-Dubz. I got on really well with the boys and we've remained friends ever since,' he wrote in his autobiography.

On his return he went straight into writing his first album. Weeks were spent at the Rollover Studios in West London, where Peter worked into the early hours, sleeping on a sofa and penning track after track with producer Ollie

Jacobs, who worked with the likes of pop sensations The Prodigy, Mis-teeq and The Chemical Brothers.

One of the pair's creations, 'Mysterious Girl', written alongside Glen Goldsmith and Philip Jackson, was chosen as his second single. With its laid-back reggae vibes and sultry lyrics, Peter, his management company and record label all agreed it was likely to be an instant hit with his plethora of female fans. While the song did well in the Pacific, reaching No. 1 in New Zealand and No. 8 in Australia, it charted only at a modest 53 in the UK.

Peter knew where they had gone wrong. Not only was it a summer song that had been released during a British winter, he was now wise to the fact his body sold a single just as much as his voice. He re-cut the single's video himself to give fans exactly the recipe he knew they wanted – steamy images of his honed torso. Hours slaving away in the edit suite saw the video for 'Mysterious Girl' feature Peter in all his six-pack glory standing beneath a waterfall. Leaving little to the imagination it also included shots of him from the video shoot in Thailand, gyrating and showing off his well-oiled muscles while singing in a crystal-blue lagoon.

When it aired on cable music channel The Box – where viewers would call up to have their favourite video played – the impact was instant and it quickly started crawling up the Billboard chart, overtaking the 30 or so American singles in its Top 40. The more it was shown, the more fans started calling in and when it finally reached No. 1, it stayed there for an astonishing 12 weeks.

After 'Mysterious Girl' originally failed to get the

recognition he'd hoped for, Peter, alongside putting out the re-cut video, also released a third single, 'Only One', from the new album, which shot straight in at No. 16. Not only that, his continued success brought an invite to appear on primetime BBC music show *Top of the Tops*, which he'd always viewed as a benchmark for knowing whether he'd cracked the UK.

'You can imagine how proud I was to call my mum and tell her that her little boy was making it big back in Britain. Even though I was thrilled to have been on the show, the performance wasn't great and the styling was dreadful!' he remembered years later.

But after that TV appearance and on the back of the single's success, the new wonder boy of pop joined Irish boy band Boyzone on their 1996 tour. While he was on the road and with its triumph on *The Box*, Peter got the call he'd wanted – 'Mysterious Girl' had gone back into the charts and this time shot straight in at No. 3.

It was a runaway success selling over 900,000 copies and after peaking at No. 2, became the biggest-selling single of the year.

Peter said in an interview with the *People* that year: 'I always wanted to succeed here. I consider it my home and it's one of the hardest markets to crack. "Mysterious Girl" getting to No. 2 and staying there for so long was a really great surprise for me.'

Two other singles, 'Flava' and 'I Feel You', came next and both topped the chart. The cash was now pouring in. Instead of £10 a gig, Peter could now command £10,000 a show. Three months after the release of his debut UK album *Natural* in October 1997 with a star-studded launch at London's Natural History Museum, he was officially declared a millionaire. He'd finally made it in more ways than one. Now the world was gripped by 'Peter Mania' and he'd started to believe the hype, perhaps (he admitted, many years later) a little more than he should.

CHAPTER FOUR
MYSTERIOUS GIRLS

The picture of a dark-haired boy being tied up and bullied by his classmates was now something of a distant memory. Peter was adored by everyone; from teenage girls to middle-aged mums – even the notoriously cruel British tabloid press were grappling for interviews and affectionately dubbing him their 'Aussie Adonis' with 'serious pecs appeal'.

'Peter Andre is the pop star who has everything. A string of smash hits, a glam image and thousands of devoted fans,' a report in the *Sunday Mail* gushed in 1996. His life had become a crazy merry-go-round of recording and promoting singles, putting on gigs, presenting TV shows, making public appearances and on top of that hours and hours of fitness training to keep his body in shape. Fortunately for Peter, despite being in a superficial industry where at his level of fame it would have been difficult to know who to trust, he had just the security net he needed and so he fell back into the arms of his family. His four brothers – whom he could rely on 100 per cent – along with manager Claire made up a close-knit entourage.

At one point he had his eldest sibling Andrew, then a marketing consultant, helping out with merchandise, Michael and Chris, his sometimes backing dancers at live shows and perhaps most crucial of all, tough Danny in charge of overseeing his security – and boy, did Peter need it. Britain's now No. 1 pin-up was attracting a whole new level of attention. Teams of police officers were being called out to his record signings as thousands of fans stampeded town centres to catch a glimpse of their idol.

'We went to a signing in Bristol and a thousand people showed up and the police had to shut down the store but nothing prepared us for what happened at the HMV store in Liverpool,' he told *Smash Hits* in 1996. 'Over two and a half thousand people turned up, 27 police officers arrived and the whole building had to be closed down. We were trapped inside for three hours – they even had to block off the street outside. I'd never seen this before, I was completely shocked.'

Although frightening, there was a definite upside to all this attention. Aside from his records flying off the shelves, women in their droves wanted to sleep with him.

'I'm the boy from Down Under that likes to go under. In fact, I'm the boy that does nothing except go under!' Peter boasted on Australia's *It's Not The Pete Doherty Show* in reference to his well-documented sex life. Hilariously, he also claimed to keep all the used underwear girls had sent him in a 'secret room' in his London bachelor pad.

By the time his album *Natural* was released in 1996 he'd had a string of affairs and tried countless times to break off his engagement with Kathy, back home in Australia. He had hinted that if their relationship had a future she'd have to move to Britain to be with him but Kathy, who was now running a ballet school, threw it back at him, saying he could just as easily return home. Peter knew that would mean career suicide and selfishly, he admitted in later years, he left the relationship as it was, terrified if they did officially split then he wouldn't be able to cope with seeing her with someone else. But it was a wonder that their relationship continued to survive as Kathy – against the odds – remained in the dark over Peter's philandering on the other side of the world.

Far from being secretive, the singer was sharing a highly promiscuous love life with newspapers claiming he had bedded over 50 women since arriving in Britain. Peter added fuel to the fire by bragging to a teen magazine after his No. 1 hit, 'I Feel You': 'I'm so passionate, I'm a hot-blooded man and addicted to sex.'

It was all true, of course. Beautiful women were throwing themselves at him and he found the affairs provided an excellent escape from the pressures of his career and messy love life back home.

'I had no respect for these girls or myself. I was rebellious and sex became my only release. If I'm honest with myself I was feeling very lost and lonely. Sex was my drug and I was addicted,' he admitted. In another interview with iconic lads' mag *Loaded* in 2006 he admitted to being a 'total whore' wherever he went: 'My manager told me not to sleep with a groupie in every town I played as I'd never get invited back. So I'd collect the girls' numbers and sleep with them on the return leg! I was basically a male slut and a total whore.'

And at every turn there was another girl for the taking, from models to fans to world-famous stars. While filming the raunchy video for 'Mysterious Girl' in Thailand he fleetingly dated its leading lady, a dark-haired dancer called Champagne. Another girl he met in a nightclub while on holiday in Cyprus, Nikki Heard, was one of the first women to come forward and spill the beans on what the pop star was allegedly like behind the headlines and between the sheets. In a derogatory interview with the *News of the World* Nikki claimed not only was Peter really vain, with black satin sheets on his bed and pictures of himself stuck on the bedroom walls of his Fulham flat, the chemistry between them was seriously lacking.

In another cruel put down, which actually only served to prove Pete wasn't an ego-maniac but had a vulnerable side too, Nikki said he was so embarrassed about his un-muscular legs that he covered them up at all times, sometimes during sex and even wore tracksuit bottoms in the bath.

She said of the first time they made love: 'We were at his flat. He had given me red roses and showered me with compliments. I was so flattered, I finally agreed to have sex with him. Peter took his top off and asked me to rub ice all over his body. Yet right in the middle he started looking in the mirror. It was a real turn-off for me. Then we had sex. He didn't even bother to undress and it was no great shakes. He managed to last 10 minutes. After that all he wanted was a quick wham-bam. What Peter liked most was drooling over his body.'

He later retaliated: 'It was only a brief fling, we met a couple of times. But that was the worst date I ever went on. I should have known better than to trust her – the food was good but that was the only thing!'

Such stories in the press didn't seem to put the ladies off though and aside from the no-strings-attached flings, Peter had fallen deeply in love with several women and the long-term relationships he was notching up were putting his emotions to the test.

One of his earlier girlfriends was *Home and Away* star Laura Vazquez, the only woman before Katie Price that he seriously contemplated spending the rest of his life with. Even during the many years Peter was sleeping around, he always knew that ultimately, like his own father, he was a family man who wanted to settle down, marry 'The One' and have a brood of children. While he believed Laura was that woman, it quickly became apparent they had met at the wrong time in their lives. The couple were introduced when Peter was just 20 and had flown back to Australia to appear on popular chat show *Tonight Live with Steve Visard*, which was being filmed in a TV studio next to the one used by *Home and Away*.

Laura, then 17, and best known for playing Sarah Thompson on the hit soap, snuck in to watch his performance with her friend and co-star who played Angel Parrish, Melissa George. Afterwards they chatted and when it became obvious they fancied each other, swapped numbers and started texting each other. 'At the time I was more famous than him but it was obvious he was going to be huge,' she told the *Sunday Mirror*. 'I'd heard all this gossip about this guy with an amazing body... From the moment we met I'd fallen for him.'

When Peter returned to Britain they stayed in touch as friends and met up if ever they were in the same country, until one day he realised his feelings ran a lot deeper and he suggested they give their relationship a go. The feeling was mutual and their on-off two-year romance, while described by Laura as 'wonderful', was far from straightforward.

Although not reported at the time, Peter was essentially her boyfriend in every way except in that he refused to consummate their relationship. To any outsider they were every inch the perfect couple – in love, with plenty of mutual interests, while Peter had been whole-heartedly welcomed into her family, having struck up a close friendship with Laura's mum. But knowing he was tempted by other women he was worried that he would hurt Laura if they fully committed to each other, while he also believed she was also too special to two-time with Kathy.

'I liked Laura and didn't want to take her virginity. If you take that from someone you have to be prepared to commit properly. I don't think she ever understood my motivations. I simply felt that she was too good to be messed about and at that point I didn't trust myself,' he admitted after their split.

Laura begged him to commit to her fully before eventually giving up and dating a member of boy band MN8. They didn't talk for six months and when he discovered a year later that Laura had married, Peter was devastated. At the time it was clearly a bitter split, with Laura publicly accusing him of being a two-timing womaniser hooked on sex.

'Peter is not the sort of guy to be satisfied with one relationship. He really cannot help himself when it comes to the girls. They just fall under his spell. When I found out he was involved with another girl, I felt hurt at first. I soon realised I was never going to change him and I know the relationship was never going anywhere.

'In a way we just drifted apart,' she revealed in an interview with the *Sunday Mirror*.

Another love had fallen by the wayside, but there were plenty more successful women grappling for his attention.

Although little was made of it at the time, Peter also dated singer Melanie Blatt for six months before she became famous with the nineties girl band, *All Saints*. As with Laura, their relationship was intense but they never slept together and Mel told Peter when they later bumped into each other that he had hurt her badly.

'I was a lot more serious about her than her about me. Funnily enough we never made love,' he admitted many years later. 'She was going through a hard time. I'm disgusted with my behaviour now but I acted like a complete arsehole. I kept hassling her because I thought I didn't turn her on.'

Usually the one in control of the destiny of his relationships, the tables were turned when he met model Charleen Edlund when his passionate love for her turned into a dangerous obsession. Peter was swept off his feet by the pretty 19-year-old from South London who had starred in make-up ads for Rimmel and Schwarzkopf, while shooting his second No. 1 smash, 'I Feel You'. The singer had handpicked her at auditions in October 2006 to play opposite him in the video after finding they shared instant chemistry.

It was just as well for the storyline required the pair to get extremely close straightaway in a number of kinky scenes, including one where Peter sensually kissed her inner thigh. The original video was deemed so X-rated and convincing that it was banned by teen music shows *The Chart Show* and *Live & Kicking* for being too explicit.

Behind the scenes, though, Peter's unmistakeable passion for the girl who was his perfect type: 'green eyes, brown hair and light coffee-coloured skin' meant he couldn't trust her and he was became increasingly possessive. Towards the end of their six-month affair he was ashamed to admit he didn't want her to leave home to go to work.

'She was working as a bargirl and often wore see-through dresses. I hated it. It was really wrong and it drove her to insanity. After six months together I was convinced she was seeing someone else. It was killing me and I've never known the truth. I never cheated on her, never even thought about it, but I was too gone – and it was wrong.'

It was halfway through his 'Mysterious Girl' 30-date European tour that he eventually called time on the relationship. One evening in his hotel room, instead of making love as they usually did, he told her it was over. They were both desperately unhappy about it but Peter knew that in order to preserve his sanity, this was the right thing to do. For the rest of the tour he refused to perform 'I Feel You' because it served as too much of a painful reminder of their time together.

Publicly blaming it on their busy work schedules, Peter told the *Sun* soon after their split: 'What we had together was perfect, it had been love at first sight. It was a heart-breaking choice for me to make because she really was the great love of my life.'

Charleen was equally complimentary about her ex in a 1997 kiss-and-tell about their love life with the *News Of The World*, saying he had seduced her with love letters, bouquets and a romantic £20,000 holiday in Barbados over Christmas.

'He can make me shiver just by stroking my hair. I'll never forget that first night together when he ran his fingers over my skin. We'd make love three times a day... the sort of lovemaking that moves you to tears. Afterwards he would hold me tight for the whole night.'

Clearly heartbroken after the split she added: 'I hope that one day we can have back what we're missing now.'

Determined not to reach such a low point again, Peter ploughed himself back into work. He was now single again and for the first time ever, even long-term girlfriend Kathy was finally out of the picture.

She had discovered his infidelity when Charleen picked up Peter's phone one day when he was having a shower and asked who she was. When Charleen told her she was his girlfriend, Kathy broke down in tears and demanded Peter be put on the phone. Deeply apologetic, the singer explained how he had tried to break it off countless times before but the thousands of miles between them had made it impossible. Feeling terrible about the way they split, he explained to the *Sun* the following year (2007): 'When I left for London, Kathy and I agreed we would get engaged when I came back and quickly marry afterwards. But things took off and marriage never happened. I've stayed in touch with Kathy, who is engaged to another guy now. Serves me right.'

Peter was now full swing into his rebellious 20s and as well as the booze, partying and endless one-night stands, his reckless ways even extended to getting an intimate piercing to enhance his pleasure in the bedroom.

He wrote in his *New!* magazine column in 2012: 'I admitted on Paddy McGuinness' show, *Mad Mad World*, last Saturday that I had my "how's your father" pierced way back in the 90s.

'I don't know what I was thinking, revealing that on national television, to be honest. I'm a nutter!

'But anyway, let's just say I won't be doing it again anytime soon. It was painful!'

It was also around this time that Peter dated one of his most famous exes – and the one who appeared to cause the most jealous rows with his future wife, Katie Price – Spice Girl Mel B. The pair had an incredibly passionate six-month affair during which she cheated on him, giving him perhaps one of his greatest life lessons in love and fidelity. 'I got played at my own game,' Peter later confessed, 'The player got played. I'd done it to girls a hundred times and now someone was doing it to me. And it hurt.'

Right from the start, curly-haired Melanie Brown, aka

Scary Spice, was out to ensnare Peter and she wouldn't take no for an answer. Despite both being incredibly famous at the time – the Spice Girls had just released their first single, 'Wannabe', which was No. 1 in 31 countries – their top-secret passionate fling managed to remain under the press radar. Mel B, who clearly wore the trousers in their relationship, orchestrated it so that although they were constantly in the limelight, the famous duo were never seen in public together long enough to confirm their affair.

To begin with, it was a game of cat and mouse. Mel and Peter met when they appeared on the same bill for a big national road tour across Britain and while rehearsing backstage one of the Spice Girls' road crew let on to the singer that she fancied him. They eventually met up after Mel B's bandmates Melanie Chisholm, Victoria Adams (now Beckham) and Geri Halliwell told Peter at the 1996 *Smash Hits* Poll Winners Party, where he was nominated for Best Male Artist, that she was crazy about him and desperate to get his phone number. Despite not getting together on the night, determined Mel B begged a record plugger for his number and contacted Peter for a date.

Peter was flattered and it was the start of an intense but bizarre fling during which Mel would call 20 to 40 times a day, sharing intimate details of her life with him but was adamant they were never to be seen out in public together. Instead, she insisted on only meeting at her apartment or a hotel room, with Peter often arriving at an agreed location hidden under a blanket in the back of her chauffeur-driven car. Even their first date was a private meal for two cooked by a chef at her luxury flat in Windsor.

Looking back it was clear Mel didn't see a future but at the time she managed to keep him hooked by telling Peter she loved him while blaming the pressures of publicity on keeping their love affair a secret. It was hardly conventional but it was easy for Pete to justify in that nothing was conventional about the world they were living in. Not only that, she was flying him across the world, once spending £30,000 on a private jet, to wherever the Spice Girls were performing so they could spend time with each other.

Peter knew something was wrong and never felt wholly comfortable with the arrangement but nothing could have prepared him for the shocking truth when it finally came out.

'She was always begging me to ring her and she would say, "I love you so much. I can't be without you." But it was all just bullshit. At the same time she was professing her love for me she went and married a dancer called Jimmy Gulzar!'

A bewildered Peter made the discovery when midway through having sex in a hotel room in Atlanta, Georgia, where Mel was recording a new track, the phone rang and it was her lawyer in London. Over the speakerphone, he said the *Sun* was reporting on its front page that Mel was divorcing Jimmy. Peter had no idea the woman in bed with him was married, let alone getting a divorce. In shock, he rolled off the bed, calmly got dressed and left. It later transpired that Mel had married Jimmy in England when Pete had made a return trip to Australia, hence him knowing nothing about it. After that there was no going back for either of them although they continued to chat as friends for months after.

Despite his personal problems, Peter's career was proving a dream come true and he was ticking off his lifelong ambitions one by one. Soon after riding high with his No. 1 hit, 'I Feel You', he performed at the World Music Awards in Monaco to an audience that included Lionel Richie, Celine Dion and HSH Prince Albert II of Monaco. The after-show party was a lavish affair held on a huge yacht with an on-board casino, helipad and a champagne reception that included caviar served off ice sculptures.

For Pete it was there that another dream was fulfilled, meeting his all-time 'ideal' woman, Halle Berry. Although he was so nervous his legs were shaking, he managed to get a photo of them together and was so proud of it that the snap appeared in the programme for his arena tour, the following year.

Peter was now mixing with the rich and famous, even his bachelor pad in an apartment block behind London's Earls Court boasted celebrity neighbours TV duo Anthony McPartlin and Declan Donnelly (Ant & Dec) and singer Dannii Minogue. But towards the end of 1996, he was finding himself more and more dissatisfied with life and increasingly tired of being in the limelight 24/7. It had been a manic 12 months during which he'd achieved four Top 40 hits, a chart-topping album and a UK tour that sold out in four hours flat. His first major arena tour was also on the horizon for the following summer and he had just been signed up as the new face of Calvin Klein underwear in a £300,000 deal. Concerned he was close to burning out, he begged his management for some time out. Claire agreed and they flew to Los Angeles.

Peter had long held an obsession with America and was fascinated by its music, fashion and culture, so coupled with the warm sunshine it was just the tonic he needed. For a few blissful months, he rented out a plush six-bedroom Beverly Hills mansion complete with Jacuzzi, steam room, swimming pool and gardens. The slice of the high life helped spur him into writing his new album *Time* and he began gaining his confidence and energy back.

Days were spent being cooked hearty meals by Claire and watching gangster movies by the pool with his brother Mike, who had accompanied him on the trip, in between laying down tracks in the studio and filming the video for his new single, 'Lonely', in Arizona.

With his upcoming *Natural* Arena Tour Pete also started looking for inspiration to make it the best show of his life and a trip to watch the Cirque du Soleil in Las Vegas had the answer. By the time the tour arrived in June 1997 he knew he'd struck gold.

The show opened with the whole arena blanketed in darkness before a countdown simulating a rocket launch worked the 10,000-strong audience to fever pitch. Peter then burst onto the stage – designed to look like a dark American backstreet – and slowly removed his black sunglasses to deafening applause. It was a massive success and none more so than the much-hyped climax to the tour – and the pinnacle of his career so far: a performance at Wembley Arena.

'It was something I'd dreamed of in every imaginable

detail since I was a young kid. I'll never forget it. I'd only ever been a support artist there. Now it was my turn to take the main dressing room with the big bathroom. At that moment I really thought I'd arrived.'

He may not have realised it at the time but behind his tough onstage exterior – the mirrored shades, rippling abs and Judge Dredd-style outfits – he was quickly unravelling at the seams. For starters his strict pre-show routine included eating just one small meal on the day of a performance alongside a punishing workout of up to 500 sit-ups in the hour running up to the show. Afterwards he would eat a specially prepared chicken pasta meal from a plastic container on the tour bus and if any part of his ritual was disturbed, he would go ballistic.

His luck with the ladies and the strong body image he'd built for himself meant the star was now knee-deep in an obsession with exercise and eating which had reached dangerous proportions. As well as rarely consuming anything nutritious, he had started drinking heavily, getting through a few bottles of wine by himself a night. A candid interview with the *Sun* in 1997 said it all.

'I've been linked with more beautiful women than Peter Stringfellow but believe it or not, I'm not the most vain guy in the world but my image is important. The last thing I want is to stop exercising then wake up one morning and discover I've got a gut that looks more like a burst accordion than a washboard. I also find that I have to watch what I eat... in fact I probably don't eat enough.'

It was after filming the video for chart-topper 'Flava' on Venice Beach in Los Angeles during the summer of 1996, a year before his arena tour, that he collapsed. Desperate to look good on-camera Peter had woken up at 4.30am to go to the gym and while on the scorching-hot set refused to eat but would instead dart into the shade to do sit-ups during breaks in filming. His concerned manager Claire managed to persuade him to eat a small amount of fish midway through the schedule, but when they wrapped 12 hours later at 3am Peter collapsed and started projectile vomiting. He was diagnosed with exhaustion and dehydration by a doctor and told he couldn't fly to Glasgow for an AIDS benefit gig with Irish boy band Boyzone the following evening.

The press back in Britain caught wind of his collapse and headlines the following morning reported not only was he ill but some claimed he was dying from AIDS and had just three months to live. Claire's business partner Sue Harris was inundated with calls from tearful teenage girls and covered for Peter in an official statement saying he'd simply been struck down with food poisoning.

The following day, Peter jetted into Birmingham for the benefit concert's second gig under a cloak. Claire told him afterwards that she would put together a proper timetable for eating and exercising to give him back control of his life but it didn't last long. Peter was taking himself too seriously and staying toned was his life. At one point his body fat plummeted to a terrifying 3 per cent, where 15 per cent is deemed healthy. Not only did he take protein shakes and his own food to his specific low-calorie requirements everywhere he went, he would only stay in hotels where the gym had the right equipment for his three-times-a-day workouts.

The situation reached almost comic proportions when on one long-haul flight Peter asked an air stewardess for a space in Business Class for a strenuous mid-air workout of push-ups and sit-ups while everyone else in the cabin was fast asleep.

Anxiety had also started to rear its ugly head again and he found himself terrified of being attacked in public.

Peter finally acknowledged something was seriously wrong when he went to watch his childhood hero Michael Jackson in the summer of 1997 perform to 80,000 fans at Wembley Stadium and insisted on leaving early. With echoes of the anxiety attacks he'd endured in Sydney before he'd left to find fame in London, Peter found himself looking over his shoulder every few minutes, worried he would be stabbed.

As if things couldn't get much worse, his next album, *Time*, which he'd written during his time in America with big name artists Coolio, Montell Jordan and The Fugees, charted a few months later at a disappointing 28. Although his previous singles, 'All About Us' and 'Lonely', had hit the UK's Top Five, Peter's fans clearly didn't like his new move towards R&B and it was to signal the beginning of the end. The press had a field day at his expense and it wasn't just his music they were mocking either. He was no longer the superhunk with 'the torso making mouths water' but the 'baby-oiled boy' who was 'Pop's Premier Plonker'.

After news of his album's disastrous chart entry Peter locked himself in his bedroom and refused to talk or eat for three days. Burnt out and knowing his record company was considering dropping him too, he felt like he was backed into a corner.

'Getting to where I thought was a safe place was top of my priority list. Crazy really, given the work I had put in to make it big in Britain and now I wanted to go somewhere else,' he admitted in his autobiography.

Everyone had started rallying against him and he knew from experience there was only one thing to do. Time to up sticks, get out of there and go back to where he felt safest: back home with his family.

CHAPTER FIVE
LOSING IT

Peter jetted straight to Bribie Island, an island off the coast of Australia, where his parents were now running a pretty boutique hotel. Some years earlier he had bought into the picturesque beachside resort with his father and it seemed the perfect place for the singer to relax and recuperate thousands of miles from the crazy life he'd left behind in London. A three-month stay would give him ample time to work out his next move.

For the first time in 10 years Peter was relieved not to wake up to a relentless itinerary of promos, gigs or training but instead mucked in with the rest of the family waiting tables, cleaning and chatting to guests. But three days in, the superstar had just started to relax and feel like a normal person again when he suffered a massive breakdown. He had sat down for dinner with his parents when seemingly out of the blue it felt as if his brain was exploding. His brothers had asked him earlier in the evening if he wanted to join them at the cinema but still feeling tired, he chose to stay behind and catch up with Savva and Thea over a steak dinner and a glass of wine. But as he picked up his sharp steak knife Peter began shaking uncontrollably. Suddenly his mind became flooded with images of himself brutally cutting his wrists and slashing his body. Dropping his cutlery with a clatter he ran sobbing to his bedroom, unable to get the horrifying, flashing images out of his mind.

'I had an inner rage that was horrific,' he explained afterwards. 'I was freaking out, yelling, screaming and shaking. I couldn't blot out the scenes flashing round my mind of me slicing my wrists and jumping out of windows.'

His frightened parents called his brothers home to help and they immediately rushed Peter to hospital, where a doctor asked if he'd ever suffered a 'psychotic episode' before. When he was later allowed home to rest he was so shaken by the ordeal that he asked his brother Mike to sleep in his bedroom overnight.

The next day he took another turn for the worse. The morning had started like any other at the hotel but by the afternoon he was gripped by yet another panic attack. The frightening episodes, which were to plague him up to 20 times a day for the next two years, had kicked in with a vengeance and suddenly he would find himself hyper-ventilating as his heart seemed to beat out of control.

It was clear the constant battle to stay at the top of the charts, the fear of being attacked and his unhealthy obsession with fitness and diet had finally pushed Pete over the edge. The only time he felt safe was when he was asleep so he started sleeping 18 hours a night. During the day he tried to keep busy by making his way through a list of chores around the hotel in between seeking help from doctors and therapists in a desperate bid to try and unravel his problems.

When months down the line none of the professionals seemed to have a solution to the 'panic disorder' he'd been diagnosed with, the singer decided it was time to look elsewhere for help. He was also feeling progressively lonely and isolated on the sunshine island and coupled with the fact he had mounting debts and little cash in the bank, Peter knew he couldn't stay in Australia for much longer.

With returning to the UK out of the question, he felt his only option was to try and crack America once and for all and with his brothers Chris and Michael in tow, he flew to New York. As soon as they touched down, Peter immediately set to work and arranged meetings with record bosses to see if he could land a contract. David Sonnenberg, boss of management label DAS Communications who managed The Fugees, a band Peter had written with before, agreed to take him on. Back in London his manager Claire tried to warn him that he was making a big mistake – explaining he would be a very small fish in a very big pond – but Peter was determined to live the 'American Dream' and no one was going to stop him.

'He became pretty obsessed with the whole America thing – he wanted to break America, he wanted to dress American, he really thought the grass was greener on the other side,' Claire admitted in an ITV interview.

Although his record sales had taken a serious nosedive back in Britain, things initially started looking up for Peter in the States. He was asked to record 'Kiss The Girl' for Disney movie, *The Little Mermaid*, which reached No. 9 in the UK chart in 1998 and his new US management appeared to be taking him seriously. They had set him up in a recording studio and asked him to write and record new tracks especially for the American market. However it wasn't long before Peter realised that perhaps Claire had been right: it was going to be a lot tougher than he'd imagined. He hadn't been signed up to do any public appearances but was being kept back by working for days on end in the studio.

It was the worst set-up possible for Pete's fragile state of mind and his panic attacks worsened as he became convinced that his career was now well and truly over. Eventually he had to come clean and tell his manager what was going on.

'I tried to bury my fears and run away from it all, but eventually it just all caught up with me and I broke down,' he told the *Mail On Sunday*. 'I simply couldn't work at all. The year before I had sold out Wembley and suddenly I couldn't get through a morning.'

He was seen by one of America's top psychiatrists, who suspected his condition was 'psychotic' and referred him to a mental hospital as an in-patient. 'I saw all sorts of psychiatrists and this one said I needed to be admitted, not because he thought I was a danger to anybody but I was a danger to myself,' Pete told ITV's *Life Stories*. 'So he put me in this ward and it was a horrible place. I remember walking in there and you'd expect to feel safe but I felt worse, not better.'

Everywhere he looked there were severely mentally ill patients, some in straitjackets, others rocking back and forth for hours on end and some so disturbed they couldn't speak. Meanwhile, Peter was trying to cope with terrifying hallucinations and at his lowest point, was even contemplating suicide.

'There were times when it was so bad that I thought, "Am I better off?" But you have to look at what's around you,' he told *OK!* magazine in 2010. 'My family were my entire life and I thought, "How are they going to live the rest of their lives? That's what stopped me."'

In the outside world it had got to the point where Peter couldn't go out of his house without having a panic attack and even crossing a road became a problem.

'Each time I had a panic attack I thought I was going to die. An attack lasts for about 25 minutes – you start hyperventilating, your heart beats at an incredible rate, your hands go sweaty, and your jaw sometimes locks.

'Basically your body goes into shock and I've had it when both my hands and jaw lock at the same time. It was really, really bad.'

Though released after a fortnight, he was far from cured.

'I spent two weeks going to group therapy, talking to people. I was then discharged and put on seriously strong medication, which actually made me worse. It was a really bad time,' the singer later told the *Daily Mail*.

Even the day he left hospital Peter was still so ill he became convinced that the taxi taking him home was about to explode. After screaming to be let out, his brothers took him to New York's Central Park to calm down, where he was hallucinating so severely he thought he could see people falling out of trees. Life was becoming unbearable. Peter developed a phobia of heights and knives, which got so severe that when eating out at restaurants he ordered dishes like spaghetti that he could eat with a fork and didn't need cutting up. When staying in hotels he also did everything he could to protect himself from harm including getting staff to lock the windows so he couldn't jump out of them.

Eventually his management decided a move to Los Angeles where the pace of life was slower might help his recuperation and Peter agreed. It was there that he met a woman who finally helped him conquer his demons.

While living in a beautiful house just off Sunset Boulevard, Peter had become firm friends with fellow Brit and international superstar Rod Stewart and his wife Rachel Hunter and one evening when his manager Claire was in town she invited them to go and watch a hot new band she was looking after, called My Town.

Rachel's sister and personal assistant Jacqui came along and she and Peter hit it off straightaway.

'I told her about the attacks, the breakdown, the medication. She told me about this therapist, Claudia Newman,' he later told the *Mail On Sunday*.

'I started seeing Claudia and she switched all the lights back on in my head: she took me off medication and just made me talk about myself, my background, my thoughts, my fears and guilt and everything. She made me look at myself, understand who I was and build myself up again.

'It became more and more clear to both of us that everything that was tormenting me stemmed from the mental trauma I had undergone during the years in Australia,' he explained further, years later. 'She helped me to see that I actually hated my work and way of life and that together they had destroyed me. Another important thing was that for the past few years I hadn't had a base to give me a sense of security. All that time I'd been living out of a suitcase. In time I closed a painful chapter in my life, I was no longer lost in my own world.'

The therapy sessions lasted about a year and finally Peter felt in control of his life. He had now split from Claire's management company after their contract ended and they agreed it would be impossible for her to manage him from London when he was so insistent that America was where he would make his fame and fortune.

Without her guidance Peter had initially felt incredibly vulnerable but determined to succeed, he met up with several managers before signing with Lou Pearlman, a famous producer who launched Backstreet Boys and *NSYNC. Lou promised to make him famous in America and set up meetings with big name sponsors Coca-Cola, Pepsi and McDonald's, who all seemed keen to be part of a huge Peter Andre launch Stateside.

But six months into the deal it was clear Lou wasn't going to deliver. Peter kept flying to Orlando for meetings, each time at his own expense, but nothing seemed to be progressing. Lou said he would only get work if he built up his body into a rippling six-pack again but Pete had ditched that image for a slick designer look with the release of his album *Time* and had no desire to return to it.

But Peter had changed. By the time he was axed by Mushroom Records in 2000, far from being panic-stricken, he was relieved. He had come to realise, through several years of therapy and his blossoming relationship with Jacqui that he was no longer desperate to be a star and was a lot happier and secure with a life no longer over-shadowed by the pressures of fame. He hadn't released a new song for almost three years and when the 9/11 terrorist attack happened in 2001, it seemed like a natural time for Peter to part company with Lou for good.

Time for a new start away from the music industry, Peter returned to Australia feeling more confident than ever.

He jetted straight back to Bribie Island and told his hardworking parents, both now suffering from ill health, to return home to Queensland while he and his three brothers would take over the running of the hotel.

'I did that for two years without taking a wage. I asked my dad to let me learn how to live on nothing. I had my own business and a house in Australia that I had built myself, so I could easily have taken a loan. It was hard for a couple of months but I had to do it, though because it was our business and it wasn't fair that Mum and Dad had to run it,' he explained later. 'They kept saying to me, "You've got to go back to England", and I was like, "No, I think it's good to have a break – people are probably sick of me.'

Fortunately for Peter he had plenty to fall back on, having received expert financial guidance from his self-made father, who had helped him invest his money wisely throughout his career. As well as squirrelling away any royalties that came from his Australian hits, Peter also had other channels of income, such as the massive sums of cash he'd made from merchandising on his tours.

'I remember one night at the Royal Albert Hall just in T-shirts I made £20,000!' he confessed in an interview later.

Like his father had done all those years ago in 1960s London, Peter had followed in his footsteps and built his own mini empire to fall back on if times hit hard. When he first got together with millionaire Katie Price in 2004 it was widely speculated that Peter was financially ruined after he fled Britain when his career flopped. But it couldn't have been further from the truth.

'When I first had success in music in the 1990s my dad begged me to invest my money. He said, "When you are young, you think money is there and it's not." So I invested in properties in Australia and I bought a bit of land in Cyprus

'My father was my saviour because the money, such as royalties, would come in from Australia and he would just invest it for me. If it had gone into my account, I'd have just spent it – he was always telling me I was spending my money before I had it.'

With his finances back on track and with his businesses flourishing Peter started to get itchy feet and three years later, the lure of singing again was drawing him back to America. He briefly moved back to New

York to start recording some new material and feeling inspired, he called up his ex-manager Claire for advice on whether he should attempt a re-launch. She told him that with the emergence of singers coming out of talent shows such as *Pop Idol* flooding the market, it still wasn't the right time.

Taking it on board, Peter decided to go back to his roots and start afresh in Cyprus, open a business and look for a record deal with a label there. The Andreas had a holiday apartment and very quickly Peter started to get himself established with a string of new projects. He bought a large plot of land so he could build his own house and went into partnership with his brother Michael in buying a gym. His sister Debbie also came on board and ran a beauty salon downstairs. It was a world away from his music career but Peter loved it.

Locals were fascinated with having a big star in their midst running the local gym and the family started raking it in. The gym was always busy and Peter even taught his own fitness classes. He also began building up his muscles again but this time was careful to keep himself in check and not let it turn into an unhealthy obsession.

All of his money was tied up in investments and although he had little disposable cash Peter felt for the first time at peace with himself. But although his new life was good he didn't want to break links with his past either. Before going to Cyprus, Peter had begged Claire to manage him again 'if anything came up'. She agreed to keep on the look-out for something that would help re-launch his career and after turning down several reality TV shows because Peter didn't feel they were 'right', including a stint on *Celebrity Big Brother*, Claire eventually took the call that would change his life all over again.

Never in a million years could Peter have predicted that appearing on the ITV show *I'm A Celebrity... Get Me Out Of Here!* would catapult him so successfully back into the limelight.

Nor that it would introduce him to his future wife Katie Price, who would become the mother of his children.

Peter agreed to fly to Britain for auditions after Claire explained the series (which drew in 11 million viewers) was like a mix of TV challenge shows *Survivor* and *Fear Factor*, with the public voting to keep celebrities in or off the show depending on their popularity. After all he'd been through, he knew he was physically and mentally up for the challenge but fears started to set in as he flew to Britain for auditions. Not only was his fate to be dictated by the public again but more seriously, he could have a panic attack in the jungle live on TV.

But Peter had a feeling that it was his destiny and he signed the contract. He also told himself that it was to be another form of therapy to help conquer those fears he hadn't yet confronted: namely heights and his overwhelming phobia of spiders.

As one of 10 celebrities living in the Australian jungle for two weeks he was set to come face-to-face with the eight-legged insects, along with a variety of live insects and other creatures, including snakes, rats and cockroaches in the show's 'Bushtucker Trials'. During their two-week stint the stars were also told they would be sleeping rough with no luxuries as they battled it out to be crowned King or Queen of the Jungle.

'It was life-changing in many ways,' he admitted afterwards. 'Career-wise – definitely, relationship-wise – definitely, and I conquered my fears. You go to therapy for years to overcome some of your fears, y'know. And in two weeks, my fears completely went.'

But even before entering the jungle in that January of 2004, Pete already had a big challenge on his hands: recognising his fellow 'celebrity' contestants. Having gone into self-imposed hibernation for three years he was so out of touch with what was going on in Britain that he didn't know who most of them were, including his future wife and Page 3 model Jordan, aka Katie Price.

'I'd never heard of a Page 3 girl named Jordan. I'd never seen her in any papers or magazines. Nor had I heard of Jennie Bond, Lord Brocket, Diane Modahl or Mike Read. The only one I had heard of was Johnny Rotten because my brothers were mad on the Sex Pistols growing up.'

As the pre-show press gathered pace in the run-up to the third series of the Ant & Dec-presented show, 30-year-old Peter was being singled out as the 'preening pretty boy' with 16/1 odds of winning.

A report in the *Daily Mail* mocked him for being in the 'remainder's bin', adding: 'Even his own website has had no news since July 2002'.

He was also described as: 'The pop star whose seven hits between 1996–98 were sold to teenyboppers too busy drooling over his six-pack to notice the music was rubbish.'

But Peter was once again so focused on proving everyone wrong that he didn't care what the critics said.

Ironically, before leaving for the jungle, Claire gave him a pep talk and said she had one important piece of advice for him and pulled out a photo of Jordan.

'Pete, stay away from her and you will get through,' she said.

Little did she know, little did anyone know, that over the next 10 years the glamour girl staring back at him would not only become his wife and the mother of his two children but the ex with whom he would have one of the most public divorces in celebrity history.

Determined Pete waded into the jungle, with neither an inkling of what the future held nor knowing what to expect – but thankful at least for being given a third chance at fame.

CHAPTER SIX

WELCOME TO THE JUNGLE

It wasn't love at first sight for Peter when he finally clapped eyes on the woman everyone was warning him against. Nor did he recognise her as the fierce-looking glamour girl from the picture.

'She looked harmless. I was expecting someone to make an entrance wearing a mini skirt so when Katie came in wearing jeans, heels and a nice polo-neck jumper I was taken aback,' Peter said of their first meeting at the luxury hotel where contestants were staying before going into the jungle.

'She had her hair in braids and I remember being struck by her green eyes and lack of make-up. There was also a vulnerability about her that intrigued me, it wasn't at all what I was expecting,' he explained years later.

'A lot of people ask if it was love at first sight but it wasn't. There was no immediate eyes-looking-across-a-crowded-room situation between us.'

79

Peter felt relieved; not only was the 'man-eater' known as Jordan not his type, she had a boyfriend and a complicated situation with her ex, footballer Dwight Yorke, the father of her disabled, two-year-old son Harvey.

Now he could concentrate on the task in hand: survive the two weeks, raise money for charity, maybe attempt to revive his music career and then retreat to his idyllic life back in Cyprus.

But Katie, the 25-year-old ambitious glamour model whose 32FF breasts had already made her a fortune, had other ideas.

Unlike Peter, who was clueless as to who she was, Katie had fancied him for years and even drooled over his photo as a teenage pop fan.

'The sexual tension between us became mind-blowing,' she told the *Sun* a month after coming out of the jungle. 'I used to fancy him – he was my pin-up and I liked him. I fought against it every single minute we were in there, but it was impossible to resist.'

Peter, meanwhile, tried to stay as true to himself as possible. As well as allowing himself a little vanity after smuggling hair wax into camp by hiding it in clingfilm between his bum cheeks, he also – being naturally more reserved – tended to watch from the sidelines.

It was immediately clear there was a contest going on between the four loudest contestants – Lord Brocket, Neil 'Razor' Ruddock, Katie Price and Kerry McFadden (now known by her maiden name Kerry Katona) – all vying for the cameras' attention.

Katie's brash over-the-top antics sometimes put him off,

Pete later confessed, but he recognised it was a front for being deeply insecure. And as the busty model kept getting picked by the public to undertake the show's increasingly unpleasant Bushtucker Trials, he felt increasingly protective towards her.

Life in the jungle wasn't easy. The stars had to sleep in hammocks or makeshift beds, food was rationed to beans and two spoonfuls of rice – unless meals were won by exhausted contestants – and the tasks themselves, known as Bushtucker Trials, were harrowing.

Although Peter wasn't picked on as much as Katie, he had his fair share of terrifying ordeals. The crew knew he hated spiders and one of his worst tasks was to put his head inside a Perspex tank filled with insects – including his worst fear, Huntsman spiders, which are known for their nasty bite.

'They did bite me in the glass tube, and I did have to take antihistamines for two weeks – which no one knew about. I came out in a massive rash all over my back when I got bitten on my neck. But I faced my fears – that's huge,' he said of his ordeal afterwards.

The rising sexual tension between Katie and Peter was now becoming obvious to everybody in between their constant bickering and cringeworthy teasing.

One day, with the temperature soaring over 30 degrees, Peter thought he would show Katie what he had to offer and stripped under a shower to reveal his rippling abs.

'I got up and walked away from everyone to a quiet spot where I could take my top off and splash some cool water over myself. Cleverly I made sure only Kate could see me strip. I know it sounds vain but I was desperate for her attention.'

But true to form, although Katie was clearly impressed and elbowed Kerry to look over, she was quick to shoot him down.

'You know, Pete, you should work on your lower abs – they're not that good. You haven't been training for a while, have you?' she asked him.

But Pete fired back: 'Get stuffed! Have you seen how flat your arse is?'

More jibes followed, with Katie joking she'd seen 'an acorn' underneath his trunks while he teased the model that her capped teeth were going black. But it was clearly just a cover for their mutual desire.

'Strangely enough, the first time we both really bonded was while we were wearing rubber gloves and shovelling shit, clearing out the bog.

'It was the first time in the jungle that we had got to do something together. And in a warped kind of way, it was romantic. It's sad, but we were both really excited, ecstatic – it was like our first date,' he told the *Sun*.

The pair were also caught canoodling on Katie's bed, in what Peter later crudely referred to as his 'tripod' moment. The model kept trying to find ways of speaking to Peter privately by asking him to meet her down by the lake where they had to take their microphones off to wash or inviting him to her bed at night.

'So I tiptoed over and slipped under the covers. I kissed her gently on the lips and ran my hand over her body. It was our first real moment of intimacy and I was aroused instantly. The acorn became an oak!

'Because it was night I thought no one could see us but what I didn't know was that some of the cameras were infrared and could pick up images in the dark.

'We held each other close before I kissed her for the last time and whispered, "Time for me to go, Katie. I love you!"'

As he crept out of her bed, the show's millions of viewers were given a full frontal of his manhood in all its glory.

The next day instead of being the loved-up woman he'd shared intimate time with the night before, Katie continued to tease him about his 'acorn', making Peter look and feel stupid. Concerned campmate Lord Brocket took him aside and told him, 'My boy, you're a nice man and I'm sad to have to tell you, you're being played.'

Her confusing behaviour also caused a stir with the press, who were accusing Katie of stringing him along to win viewers' votes.

The night before Katie was voted off the show, a fed-up Peter confronted her and asked if she was playing games. She shrugged it off, saying she refused to talk about it in front of the cameras.

Not having had the chance to make up with him before being evicted, Katie – who immediately dumped her millionaire boyfriend Scott Sullivan on being booted off the programme – yelled back into the celebrity camp as she was cheered off the show: 'Tell Peter I said yes and I miss him!'

When Peter was finally thrown out himself after coming a respectable third – with Kerry Katona being crowned that year's Queen of the Jungle – he had absolutely no idea what the future held: would Katie still be interested? What did the public think of him? Did he have another chance at a music career? Having remained on the show until its final day at least it proved to him that he wasn't the write-off everyone had thought he was at the start.

Thankfully, waiting for him on the bridge as he left was manager Claire – and she had brilliant news for him. Already in the pipeline were a new album deal, a UK tour and even a calendar – and, to his astonishment, she was now managing Katie, too.

'I've seen a different side to her,' Claire told him, 'She's a really sweet girl and I think she genuinely loves you. She asked me to manage her and I agreed.'

Stunned by the turnaround, Peter was whisked off to be reunited with his proud parents, Savva and Thea, and yet another surprise was in store: Katie was there waiting to greet him, too.

She had spent the past 24 hours looking back at the show's footage and having seen Peter professing his love for her to their campmates, she now knew he was 100 per cent genuine. As they hugged in front of the cameras, he whispered to her: 'You see, I told you I wasn't lying.' But as much as he was overjoyed that she was now back in his arms, Peter immediately wasn't keen on the heavily made-up girl in front of him with little trace of the natural jungle allure he'd fallen for. He quickly realised it was Katie Price he was in love with, not her wild, big-breasted alter-ego Jordan – a point he would reiterate over and over for many years to come.

In a post-*I'm A Celebrity...* interview he said: 'Katie's an awesome girl, I just hope she realises she doesn't have to be Jordan.

'She can be herself and people will hopefully see that side of her. I saw it, so did everyone else in camp. I don't want anything to do with all that wild-child stuff. She put on a front, always teasing me and trying to act all hard, like kids at school. But they always say when girls are horrible to you, it means they fancy you.'

They fancied each other alright but Katie's feelings seemed to run incredibly deep for someone she'd only known for a fortnight. Within hours of the show's closing credits and at its after-show party, she asked Peter to marry her.

'The day he got evicted, I asked him to marry me. We weren't even alone – his brother Danny was there, too. We were all in his hotel room and I said: "Peter, I need to ask you something beginning with an M." He couldn't work it out, so I said: "Marriage. I want you to marry me." He thought I was drunk, so he said: "Yeah, whatever."

'We only had a few hours together before we were separated to go off and do interviews but the next day he called me and said: "Did you mean it, what you said?" I said I did. But he still wouldn't believe it. He said we needed time to get to know each other, outside the jungle. But I knew I did mean it and I asked him every day for the next three months,' she admitted.

Peter was just as infatuated with Katie but was so taken aback by the intensity of her nature and still worried she was playing games that he insisted they take it slow. Not only that, his career was taking off and the re-launch of his single, 'Mysterious Girl', meant a hectic schedule of endless TV and radio interviews and public appearances.

Their now-joint manager Claire also advised that keeping their romance under wraps would strengthen their relationship without public scrutiny. It also proved an equally clever ploy in maintaining interest in their burgeoning romance at fever pitch.

Newspapers and magazines were buzzing with gossip and snaps of the pair stepping out in a string of 'secret' trysts, including a birthday dinner for Peter's 31st birthday at smart London restaurant Hakkasan, a Valentine's Day love-in at The Cavendish hotel and a night out at nightclub Pangaea, where Peter added fuel to the fire by waiting in their limo outside until Katie was safely inside.

Behind the scenes their relationship was coming on in leaps and bounds. Having slept with scores of lovers in their time and with all their talk of being 'desperate' to bed each other, it was a shock to everyone that they waited a whole month to have sex. But according to the couple it was worth waiting for.

'I've slept with a lot of women but with Katie I knew it was special, it was sensational,' he told the *Daily Mirror*. 'Seeing Katie naked for the first time was even better than what I expected. That night we made love for hours, climaxing with the most intense orgasm I've ever experienced. We looked at each other and it was so intense I couldn't believe it was real.' True to her glamour-girl image Katie meanwhile described the occasion in boorish detail to a newspaper as: 'We were like two wild animals, he was everything I had expected and longed for. Those jungle frustrations just came rushing out!'

The pair spent the next month in a hotel getting to know each other and were chaperoned by management wherever they went.

Despite holding back romantically, Pete wasn't slow to take advantage of his new status as a singer and back in the media spotlight his career was scaling new heights. It was as if he'd been thrown back to the nineties and his very public and traumatic fall from grace had never happened. In a £1million deal with record label East West the re-launch of his 1996 smash hit 'Mysterious Girl' a month after leaving the jungle stormed to the top of the charts.

It was in no small part thanks to Radio 1 DJ Chris Moyles, who ran a tireless campaign to get it released while Peter was on the hit ITV1 show.

The single, with a portion of the profits going to charity, not only took the top slot but entered the Guinness Book of Records for the number of times it was released before hitting No. 1.

His follow-up song, 'Insania', reached No. 3 in June after the track became a major talking point in the jungle, with Peter singing excerpts from it around the campfire.

Although the cheesy pop song was a hit with the public, in later years Peter was less than complimentary about his handiwork.

'That track continues to haunt me,' he groaned. 'At the time I wasn't keen to have it released. I wanted to start afresh and become a credible songwriter but "Insania" was what people wanted. It was my fault for going into the jungle and singing my way through the weeks I was in there. Anyway it sold, whether you liked it or hated it; it was a winner.'

Disappointingly his album, *The Long Road Back* released later that month, only reached No. 44 in the British album charts. But with his music career back on track Peter spent that summer performing for fans on the road. This time around it was a completely different experience. Gone was the drinking, endless women and a fitness obsession out-of-control of the nineties – the 'Insania' tour marked a new and grown-up Peter.

Not wanting to be pictured apart and doing everything she could to support him, Katie and her profoundly disabled son Harvey joined him on the UK road trip. They were now looking like a fully functioning and devoted family and it was during this time that Peter's bond with Katie's eldest son was cemented.

Harvey was born with a multitude of problems including Septo-optic Dysplasia, which causes blindness and a growth hormone deficiency; Prader-Willi syndrome, a genetic disorder leaving him prone to obesity and diabetes; as well as Attention Deficit Hyperactivity Disorder (ADHD) and autism. Although life with Harvey was sometimes challenging, Peter quickly fell in love with the tot's infectious personality and inquisitive nature. Indeed it was the start of a life-long relationship with the boy, who Peter, to this day (and even after his divorce from Katie), still regards as his own. With Harvey's real father, footballer Dwight Yorke, out of the picture, it also gave Peter a chance to play Dad before the birth of his firstborn Junior, which wasn't too far away.

'I learned how to become a father before I became a biological dad and that was all thanks to Harvey, or "H" as I love to call him.

'I've never forgotten those special moments that I spent with him before Junior and Princess came along. He taught me so much. I love him to bits and I always will,' he said.

Even with the demands of his heavily scheduled tour, Peter made time for Harvey. Popping out to the shops, an observer said: 'While Jordan nipped to the shops he pushed Harvey round the block to keep the baby amused or get him off to sleep. And when she came back it wasn't as if he was in a hurry to hand him back to her. He seemed happy to play Dad.'

What no one realised at the time was that Peter had already secured his position in Harvey's life – by secretly proposing to Katie three months after meeting in the jungle.

'In the past I'd vetoed never to date a woman with a child but I'd also vetoed blonde hair and silicone implants. All that had changed. I loved everything about Katie and I was willing to accept every part of her life,' he wrote after their wedding. Certain she was 'the one' and having promised to propose in a 'traditional and romantic' way on the proviso she'd stop asking him several times a day for his hand in marriage, Peter finally got down on one knee on her 26th birthday.

Surrounded by a dozen roses laid out in the shape of a heart in a Leeds hotel room he asked her to marry him and presented her with a £5,000 sparkling ring. Earlier that evening he had treated her to a meal at lavish London hotel

The Savoy and a matinee performance of *The Lion King* before dashing to the northern town where he was due to perform that night.

They didn't officially announce their engagement until October and kept it completely secret, denying every whisper marriage was on the cards. The few people to know about their happy news in those intervening months included their joint manager Claire and a smattering of close family members.

While Peter told Katie's mum Amy several weeks before popping the question and showed her the ring for her approval, the singer didn't announce the engagement to his parents until they flew out to Cyprus, two months later.

They had reportedly been cautious of their son's new lover and while Savva had been unimpressed with the way she treated Peter in the jungle, telling him Katie was 'bad news', his mother Thea had warned her son never to bring her into their house. So it was with great trepidation that they flew to the Andreas' holiday home in August.

Rumours were rife that the couple's trip to Cyprus, where they were also photographed by *OK!* magazine for a feature on their first holiday together, was so they could take part in the Greek 'Loyasmeni' tradition, where a couple seek permission from their parents to marry.

Although the reports weren't too wide off the mark, it was too late for Savva and Thea to lend their input in deciding whether she was the right woman for their son – but with Peter unmistakably happy for the first time in many years, they welcomed Katie with open arms. Not only that, although Peter's parents may have struggled to accept her career choice as a glamour girl, their future daughter-in-law had many attributes which they admired – she was hard-working, driven, self-sufficient and intent on having a large family like their own.

Plans for their future were now in full swing. Peter had already moved into Katie's sprawling run-down mansion she'd bought in East Sussex, having struck a deal that they would decorate it together while he would contribute financially to their new life together by building a family home on the plot of land he owned in Cyprus.

It was clear Katie was willing to embrace their Greek heritage and it put the family's relationship on a whole new footing.

Back in the UK, there was still the odd suggestion the couple were together for the publicity, even after confirming their engagement later that year, which clearly irritated Pete.

'People do say me and Katie are just a publicity stunt. Well, it has been ten months, we're getting married – so I want an Oscar. I love her, it's simple really.'

It wasn't as if Katie was playing it cool either – unabashed and clearly smitten she was revealing personal details about their life together at every given opportunity. After a holiday to the Maldives and clearly surprised by her new settled-down lifestyle, she laughed: 'We play Scrabble and gin rummy and I love it! Usually with guys, I've just wanted to go clubbing, always on the lookout for something better, but with Pete I don't have to go out. I'm happy to stay in and play cards. It's nice for the first time it's not all about sex. That's a big part of it, but I don't feel like I have to do it.'

Contrary to his bachelor image of the nineties, Peter's new status as father and devoted fiancé seemed to be going down well with his millions of female fans too and the hysteria of yesteryear at his concerts and signings was back in full force.

He was also keen to ditch the 'beefcake' tag, publicly declaring his former six-pack image as threatening and claiming these days he would choose coffee with friends over knocking back protein shakes in the gym. 'I've made a comeback nobody thought was possible,' he told *The Razz*. 'I don't want to sound like I loved myself back then but I had an image that was threatening or intimidating to people who just want to enjoy life. When you train your arse off, people think it's implants; when you prove that it's not, they say it's vanity; when you decide not to work out anymore, you've let yourself go. I thought, you know what? I'll never please everybody and what ultimately makes me happy is to go out with my friends, have a coffee or go to a bar for a drink to relax. That's the image I portray now.'

Not only was he enjoying success as a solo artist, it was also clear that Peter and Katie worked just as well professionally as they did personally and in October they were signed up for the first of their many reality TV shows.

The Page 3 star – whose saucy image under manager Claire's guidance was currently undergoing an overhaul – had already appeared on ITV's *Hell's Kitchen* as well as in the video for Peter's third single of 2004, 'Love You The Right Way'.

Shot in black and white, the shoot saw the couple writhing on a bed and beach, with Katie swapping the tarty image that made her famous for a sexier, softer look in white bikini and open-fronted shirt.

Cameramen had been following the pair since they left the jungle and in a £1million deal with ITV in October the launch of their own TV show, *When Peter Met Jordan*, was born. It was a coup for the channel, which billed it in a press release as being like the fly-on-the-wall hit MTV show *The Osbournes*, which featured the day-to-day home life of Black Sabbath singer Ozzy and his family.

'The show will be must-see TV. People will get to know the truth about their relationship. ITV1 are really excited because it's going to be massive,' a source told the *Daily Mirror*.

All eyes were now on the celebrity couple and they flew to Miami, followed by the cameras, for an engagement celebration cruise with close family and friends. They confirmed their wedding would take place the following year.

Back in Blighty, and just over a year after meeting in the jungle, Pete was about to embark on the biggest challenge of his life: fatherhood. Junior was born on 13 June 2005 and his world was knocked sideways.

'I've experienced love and I've experienced happiness but the feeling that was unlocked the moment I saw my baby boy was saved for that moment. I could never, ever explain that feeling – that love, that joy.'

It hadn't been a planned pregnancy and although Peter had always been desperate to become a father, nothing prepared him for their shock discovery.

'One night we were lying in bed and Katie pulled out a testing kit. Neither of us thought there was the remotest chance she was pregnant, so we didn't take it too seriously. Then suddenly she gasped, "Pete, is that a cross in the middle? Then she screamed, "Pete, I'm pregnant!"'

Jokingly telling her to 'stop pissing about', a stunned Peter made her do a further nine pregnancy tests and as the line grew darker each time, reality started to hit home. The singer was initially disappointed that Katie had fallen pregnant before they were married because he had always shared his parents' religious and traditional views of doing things the 'right way' but he felt mature enough to take on the challenge.

He explained later to the *Sun*: 'I really want to get married as soon as possible after the baby. Ideally for me, we would have got married before we had a child. It's the wrong way round, but you know, these things happen.'

The couple didn't publicly announce the news until March, when Katie was five months pregnant. There were several reasons for keeping it a secret. Firstly, Peter's third single since the jungle, 'The Right Way', wasn't doing particularly well and had only reached No. 14 in the charts. With ticket sales for his upcoming tour not looking like the expected sell-out either, Katie – who had never attempted a music career before – was now emerging as the singer of the family.

She had chosen to put herself forward to represent Britain in the Eurovision Song Contest. Determined to succeed, she was convinced that if people knew she was due to give birth just a few weeks before the competition's final in Kiev that May, her chances would be ruined.

There was also the second and far more serious concern that the baby could inherit the same problems as Katie's first child Harvey, who is not only severely autistic but was also born blind due to an underdevelopment of his optic nerves. Understandably they wanted to get the all-clear from pre-natal scans before making the big announcement.

In between secret hospital appointments, Katie was gearing up for a televised *Pop Idol*-style contest in which she hoped to be picked as the British entry. But just a few days before the show, her cover was blown. Appearing on ITV's *GMTV* to perform her song, 'Not Just Anybody', in a tight white mini skirt, her tell-tale bump was unmistakeable.

The breakfast show's phone lines were immediately flooded with scores of excited viewers and although initially denying it, speculation had reached such fever pitch that by the afternoon they were forced to confirm the news.

In a statement, Peter said: 'We apologise for not confirming this information earlier but we have been awaiting the all-clear from a scan, which was only confirmed at lunchtime today, that the baby is well and healthy. This was of particular importance due to the health complications with baby Harvey. The new baby is due this summer. We are all looking forward to the new addition to the family and we are extremely happy.'

A few days later and much to Katie's annoyance her dreams of a singing career were over when on the night of the TV sing-off she was pipped at the post by up-and-coming singer Javine Hylton, who was chosen to be Britain's Eurovision entry.

She wasn't the only one either. Peter's music career was also looking decidedly rocky with the news that he had been ditched by Atlantic Records and faced being a stay-at-home dad just three months before the birth.

A source told the *Daily Mirror* in March: 'Pete was devastated but he doesn't plan to give up. The money he and Jordan make from glossy magazine photo spreads will keep the coffers swollen.'

But despite the downward turn in his career, Peter was madly in love and it marked a period of domestic bliss. With the countdown to the birth in sight, the couple started 'nesting' and while Katie's calorie-friendly craving was ice, Peter began piling on the pounds as he cut back on training and honed his cooking skills instead, specialising in a range of homemade take-away style meals. Their pre-natal classes consisted of staying at home in the evenings watching TV shows on the Discovery and National Geographic channels. Pete was so absorbed in impending fatherhood, he even postponed his upcoming tour until November to ensure being present at his firstborn's birth. His management explained in a statement: 'Peter has been to L.A. to record new tracks over the past few weeks which he promises to perform on tour in November. He is also in talks with various record companies and a new single is planned. After recently announcing his and Katie's exciting news, Peter is taking his family commitments seriously and wants to make sure he is at the birth.'

It was just as well. Katie delivered their baby four weeks early and Peter was by her side all the way. Although only weighing in at 5lb 13oz on the morning of 13 June 2005,

Peter's son was perfect, had no health issues and the instant bond between father and son was unmistakeable.

His parents were equally proud and having felt the rush of love for his own son, Peter finally understood his relationship with his strict but extremely caring father. Savva himself had broken down in the hospital, where his parents had joined Katie's mum Amy to offer the couple support during the birth.

For the first time in Peter's life he saw his father cry and was so overcome with emotion he had to walk away from the cameras, who were filming the life-changing event for Peter and Katie's new reality show.

But for Katie, it was a very different story. While everyone else seemed to be overcome with emotion, the following months saw her battle severe post-natal depression which meant she was slow to develop a bond with the baby. In turn, it heaped a great deal of pressure on their relationship.

'I was thrown into fatherhood with a bang as it became more apparent over time that there was a problem with Katie bonding with the baby. Katie seemed unable to be close with him and I needed to fill that gap. We'd row over how he should be brought up and the depression meant that she'd blame me for things that weren't my fault. Our relationship was okay but it was down to me to try and hold things together.'

Although arguments are part and parcel of the process that parents face in bringing up children there was one thing they did agree on – his name. Peter wanted to follow the Greek tradition of naming a child after its grandparents and since Katie wasn't keen on his father's name Savva, which is Greek for Sabbath, they plumped on Junior Savva Andre instead.

But life behind the scenes became increasingly tough and in the face of adversity and with a 'very difficult situation' evolving at home, Peter put on a brave face and told the *Daily Mail* soon after the birth: 'He's beautiful and healthy and looks just like me. We are the happiest people in the world.'

Peter and Katie managed to struggle through the dark days and together they were conquering the early stages well in the circumstances. Katie too wasn't ungrateful for the help and she heaped praised on her husband-to-be in the months following for being 'a really good hands-on Dad', adding: 'He treats Junior and Harvey the same, which is really important. If any guy couldn't accept Harvey, they can forget being with me. He's part of me. We'll have more kids but I want to enjoy Junior first.'

Peter was now very much the picture of a man who had come home at last and the scene was set for their perfect marriage in which they could prove their doubters wrong. And there was no question it was going to be lavish.

'I want a big, Disney wedding but not like Posh and Becks, that was pathetic,' Katie told *OK!* magazine after having appeared at No. 8 in that year's *Sunday Times* Rich List, 'I want a fairytale wedding like Cinderella, with baby blues and pinks.

'I want to make the Guinness Book Of Records for the longest train in the world!'

And so the wedding wheels were put in motion.

Three months after the birth of his first child and true to his Cypriot roots, Peter's lifelong dream of being a married family man would finally become a reality.

CHAPTER SEVEN
TROUBLE AND STRIFE

It was on a shopping trip with the kids to Toys R Us that Peter realised the true extent of Katie's fantasy wedding dream. Dragged to an aisle filled with dolls she grabbed a pink Barbie and Ken horse and carriage set off the shelf and squealed: 'This is what I want our wedding to look like!' Ever tolerant, devoted Peter bought the plastic toy and gave it to their wedding planner, who set about making her dreams come true.

Aside from the model's vision of an all 'glitz and glam' affair, Peter was determined to put his own 'masculine' stamp on the day too.

'Katie had this picture of the wedding in her mind – tacky to some but I'd say it was more fairytale. She was still suffering from postnatal depression. The stress was becoming incredible and we were having the worst arguments. I wanted there to be a lot of ivory and a lot more masculine colours. I didn't want it to be all pink, for goodness sake! Other than that, I agreed with most of what was said,' he confessed years later.

As the wedding wheels were put in motion every step of the process was captured on camera for the latest instalment of their ITV reality show, *Jordan and Peter: Marriage and Mayhem*, which was pulling in top ratings. Peter and his fiancée were now close to reaching national treasure status and a measure of just how popular they had become was the £1.75million fee *OK!* magazine paid them for the rights to their wedding pictures. It was over double what the glossy publication had paid out to Hollywood stars Michael Douglas and Catherine Zeta-Jones a few years before, while David and Victoria Beckham had accepted a paltry £1million in comparison.

As if the pressure of organising the 'celebrity wedding of the century' wasn't enough, the build-up to the big day was fraught with arguments and stress too.

'I really thought at one point, Why the f**k am I getting married? I'm trapped in a shell. I don't know whether I'm coming or going. Those few months after Junior was born and getting married were difficult,' Peter once confessed.

In between choosing colour schemes and tasting canapés, he had to deal with Katie's postnatal depression, the stress of a newborn and just a month before the nuptials his stepson Harvey was rushed to Great Ormond Street Hospital with a mystery illness. Katie kept a three-week bedside vigil as doctors tried to work out what was wrong with the toddler, whose growth hormone problem appeared to be putting a massive strain on his heart.

She told *OK!* magazine at the time: 'I don't know

exactly what's wrong with him, but he is very ill. It's very serious. He will be in hospital for a long time. Something serious will happen if they don't work out what's wrong with him.'

With the wedding only weeks away, last-minute planning meetings were being held in the hospital canteen. At one point, with Harvey showing no sign of improvement, it was touch and go whether the nuptials would go ahead at all. Faced with the reality that Harvey's string of conditions meant he could be hospitalised at any point in the future, the couple made the decision to go ahead with the September ceremony regardless, agreeing it would be as good a time as ever.

Katie's postnatal depression was also taking its toll on Peter, although you would never have guessed from his public smile and the upbeat pre-wedding interviews he kept dishing out.

'Her depression and mood swings caused a lot of problems,' he confided years later. 'A distance developed between us and it was something I hadn't encountered before. But I wanted to stick by her, because I knew it was a phase.'

Even that comment vastly underplayed the gravity of the situation going on behind closed doors. Soon after Junior's birth he discovered Katie's mood had plummeted so low she had turned to illegal drugs in a desperate bid to feel better. After one binge she was left on the brink of suicide after realising it could tear their already-rocky relationship apart. The model, who has always refused to name the drug, confessed in her autobiography, *Jordan:*

Pushed to the Limit: 'After I'd taken it I thought, "this feels good" and I took some more. But then the drug took over. My heart seemed to be racing fast, I felt hot and started to panic... "Oh my God, had I overdosed? Was I going to die?"'

When Peter found out what she'd been up to he was rightly worried and according to Katie threatened to leave her. Upset, the mum-of-two drove off into the night and momentarily considered ending her own life.

'I seriously thought, "Shall I end it all now? Drive into this wall and kill myself?"'

Katie's state of mind and out-of-control behaviour was incredibly tough for both of them but whatever had happened that night the pair chose to ride out the difficult time together. Peter, meanwhile, was doing a very good job of putting on a brave face, despite further clues that behind all the talk of diamonds and tiaras their relationship was taking the strain. Firstly, he was banned from having a stag do because Katie didn't trust him. In an interview with *New!* magazine in 2010 a then disillusioned Pete admitted: 'I wasn't allowed a stag do! I never had one. I was told if I was even so much as pictured with another girl – even if she was just a fan or whatever – the wedding would be off. So I chose the wedding!'

His future wife, however, allowed herself a hen party with her girlfriends, which ended up being a modest daytime bash in a health farm, although a boozy trip to Majorca had been planned. Harvey's illness meant she wanted to remain close at hand.

'Katie's was just a daytime thing with girls, so that was

different apparently,' he added. 'When you're in love, you just go along with stuff, don't you?'

Peter's previously wild sex life had also taken a nosedive during Kate's pregnancy and with her postnatal depression any chemistry between them seemed to fizzle out altogether. She had also been prescribed anti-depressants to combat her mood swings, which lowered her sex drive even further, leaving them both strangers in the bedroom.

'Before, it had been wild and passionate exchanges. Now it was as if she was a totally different person. It did cross my mind that she'd gone off me or was interested in someone else. Then I thought it was me. It went on for what felt like an eternity. But I never argued with her about it and it never became an issue,' he insisted.

Instead, Peter kept in constant touch with his older brothers, talking through everything with them as he had done as a teenager. His family still continued to provide the emotional crash mat that he'd now become so reliant on. He also started training again, taking out his frustrations on a punch bag in their gym at home. On the plus side, the post-baby paunch he'd developed from comfort eating during Katie's pregnancy started to disappear.

Outside their family bubble, speculation about the wedding had reached fever point and when 10 September 2005 finally arrived, the promised Cinderella wedding didn't disappoint. Despite the fraught run-up, Peter loved every minute. Even after his divorce, he said of the day: 'It was magical and when I took those vows I meant every word. In many ways looking back, what Katie and I had was crazy love, but when I married, I married for love: I married for life.'

It was indeed a day fit for a prince and princess, albeit it a reality TV version of a royal bride and groom, as die-hard fans lined the street leading to Highclere Castle in Newbury, Berkshire, where the ceremony took place. Flags along the main road emblazoned with: 'Congratulations Peter and Katie' hung over a police cordon while news helicopters hovered above to catch a glimpse of Katie making her grand entrance in a pumpkin-style horse-drawn carriage.

Over 100 guests made their way to the romantic castle, now famous as the stately home used in ITV drama *Downton Abbey,* with a string of celebrities including footballer Paul Gascoigne, former BBC Royal correspondent and jungle pal Jennie Bond and soap star Jennifer Ellison.

True to her Barbie dream, Katie was dressed in a pink tulle and satin gown studded with pink crystals, designed by Isabell Kristensen, with a seven-metre train and topped off with a foot-high pink tiara. Peter, meanwhile, wore a more conservative ivory suit by the same designer made of Venetian wool, with a glittering waistcoat studded with Swarovski crystals.

Three-year-old Harvey was well enough to walk his mum down the aisle while baby Junior was looked after by the rest of their family.

A civil ceremony was held in the castle's library, followed by a blessing in the Secret Garden. The lavish reception held in a marquee was bedecked with two thrones decorated with lilac and pink flowers, a 10-foot chandelier and bay trees adorned with pink feathers and crystals. Guests, including Katie's bridesmaids *I'm A Celebrity...* winner Kerry Katona and Girls Aloud star Sarah Harding, dined on foie gras and lobster served up by waiters singing opera. Such flamboyancy was obviously ridiculed in the press, with some branding it the 'chav wedding of the year' but Katie stuck up for their every decision.

Peter even admitted afterwards that he had undergone Botox in a bid to make it the most perfect day possible. In a joint interview with TV host Jonathan Ross, Katie said: 'I had Botox. I loved it. When I have more of the stuff I'll tell the world; Peter did too.

'I don't care what people thought of my dress. I used to look at fairytale books and we worked our b******s off to get our dream wedding. I couldn't stop crying.'

While Peter nodded along at the time, he has since revealed that if he was to tie the knot again he would want a low-key affair with a lot more input: 'If I am ever to marry again things will be very different. I am an easy-going guy but I'd like a little more say in the planning and something not so showy.'

And to begin with married life started out well, despite Katie's admission that they didn't have sex on the night of the wedding but unromantically ate crisps in bed before turning in for an early night.

'I was too knackered. And so was he. We were so hungry we had a crisp sandwich in bed. But we did consummate the marriage on the Sunday morning,' she told the *Sun* newspaper afterwards.

After a family honeymoon in the Maldives, along with Katie's mum Amy to look after the two children, it was back to business. Their life together was now well documented with cameras following them everywhere for their highly successful warts-and-all TV series. Katie's string of projects included launching a new underwear range and a fitness DVD, while Peter started planning their next joint venture – a duet album.

Life seemed to be back on track and better than ever. Everything Peter and Katie said or did seemed to make the news and they appeared to have a genius for turning every element of their lives into fodder for an adoring public.

The couple were constantly snapped out together projecting a variety of images – the devoted family at the cinema, the newlyweds enjoying a date night at a London restaurant and the jealous lovebirds rowing in a nightclub after Katie told a crowd she fancied X Factor winner Shayne Ward.

Peter's sex life was restored to its sizzling glory and it seemed the key to their success was letting everyone in on every aspect of their lives – there were to be no secrets.

'Our sex life is good. And we had fun on our honeymoon,' Katie divulged to Heat magazine. 'We're addicted to St Tropez tans too. We both lie there in bed next to each other, all tanned up. We're like a pair of hot dogs.'

Rows were also a part of their public image and although some speculated their marriage was already rocky, the couple defended their bickering by saying it made them strong. In one interview they ribbed each other over the merits of curvy women against skinny ones, who cooked the better potatoes and whether Peter had more stamina in the bedroom.

Asked if their arguments were anything to worry about, Katie replied: 'Every time people see us on TV, even on something like *This Morning*, we bicker and argue. We're just so used to the cameras that we are completely ourselves. We're not putting on an act. You get other celebrity couples who don't seem real. You're always thinking, "Is it going to last?" But we do normal, everyday things and people can relate to that.'

Even the couple's finances were publicly scrutinised, with Peter admitting he asked Katie for a pre-nuptial agreement before marrying so she knew they were doing it for love. Even though it was widely known by that point that Peter had plenty of his own cash and didn't need to rely on his millionaire wife for handouts, he always felt the need to quieten the doubters. The renewed speculation was also partly due to one of Peter's exes, air stewardess Mala Burns, who claimed to have met him in secret before the couple's big day and didn't believe he was marrying for love.

'I truly believe he's partly with her for the money and the fame. I think part of Pete does love Jordan but I think he loves the money and fame just as much,' she insisted.

But the claims needed to be taken with a pinch of salt since she only came out of the woodwork after Katie banned her from the nuptials and sniped Peter had only ever dated her for cheap airfares. Indeed contrary to speculation that Peter had little financially to offer the relationship, the singer was actually enjoying their honeymoon period designing Katie the £3.5million holiday home in Cyprus he'd promised to provide in the early days of their relationship. He was also snapped flying his new wife to the holiday island to excitedly check on the progress of their 'pink palace' being built on the piece of land he'd bought just outside popular resort Larnaca as a bachelor.

His plans for the future didn't stop there either. Peter was already desperate for a bigger family, like the one he'd grown up in. He admitted four months after their wedding day that they were trying for another child and sharing her husband's desire, Katie confessed to *More!* magazine: 'We'd like to have a little girl. I'd have to call her Pink or Princess, because she'd be my princess.'

But just around the corner Peter's famous family was about to hit the headlines for all the wrong reasons when the two children were at the centre of a terrifying kidnap plot. He'd had death threats in the past, been beaten up even, but this time it wasn't just him facing the very real dangers of life in the celebrity spotlight, his kids were being threatened too.

'Until that point I'd never been caused to worry. As far I was concerned nothing could touch us. But in April 2006 a threat was made to my family and I realised just how vulnerable we really are. I've got to be honest with you, I was frightened – it was like something from a movie,' he revealed.

The first he knew of it was when a detective knocked on the door to their home in Maresfield, East Sussex and told a terrified Pete that Scotland Yard had foiled a plot to snatch either Harvey, three, or tiny 11-month-old Junior for a £1million ransom. The couple immediately cancelled everything in their schedule including a charity ball and a trip to Miami as they turned their mansion into an ultra-safe fortress with 24-hour security, bullet-proof windows and CCTV cameras. A source told the *Daily Star* at the time: 'Peter is really shaken up. They can't believe anybody could be so vicious. It's horrible because their lovely home feels like a prison now. There are police everywhere and bars on the windows. Katie's even thinking about getting firearms.'

Although the threat of kidnapping was prevented by police, the repercussions of the incident meant Peter had to completely review the way he conducted his life. Having grown up in a tight-knit beach community in Australia, his own family's life couldn't have looked more different. Top cops gave him lessons in counter-surveillance, where he learnt how to deal with people watching or following him, and he was given a special direct telephone line to the police if he ever felt threatened.

While he knew it had to be done, it reminded him of the anxiety he had experienced in the early days of his career when due to death threats and obsessed fans he had to remain vigilant at all times. It wasn't a nice place to be.

'When you're driving, you check your rear-view mirrors to see if anyone is following you. When you go round a roundabout and you think someone is following you, you go round twice or take a different exit. These are things I'd never had to do before. Unfortunately you have to have your wits about you or you're finished. Once again, I was looking over my shoulder,' he explained.

Tough as it may have been, the showbiz duo couldn't put their careers on hold forever and with their popularity soaring, they put the finishing touches to their anticipated album of love duets, *A Whole New World*, which was released towards the end of 2006. When the charity single of the same name was released for BBC Children In Need and the pair hit the promotional tour, in between Katie promoting a new lingerie range for supermarket chain ASDA, Peter made it clear how successful the Katie and Peter brand had become.

On a PR trip to Scotland, he told an interviewer: 'Believe it or not I have a lot of property now. I've started to manage property in Australia and Cyprus and I'm wanting to start upping my portfolio in the UK. I've already started building an empire and I want to make it bigger and better.'

The album, which featured 12 covers of pop classics including 'Endless Love' and 'Don't Go Breaking My Heart', was mocked in the press on the back of Katie's singing voice and her failed attempt at Eurovision. Nevertheless it reached an encouraging No. 8 in the UK charts. It wasn't a bad result for an album that Peter had originally recorded privately with Katie and hadn't intended for public release until record company Sony BMG caught wind of it and signed them up.

It looked like it was going to do well too when it went Gold after 100,000 copies were shipped to high street stores. However in a humiliating twist 40,000 albums were later found rotting in a barn in Hertfordshire, which had allegedly been returned by shops after proving impossible to sell.

When later dropped by the record company due to poor sales, as ever, Peter and Katie put a positive spin on it. The couple maintained they had never expected the album to transform them into an international singing duo and as well as being a bit of fun it had more importantly raised cash for charity. Speaking of the single and her Eurovision bid, Katie said: 'I was diabolical – it's the worst thing I've ever done. It would of course be nice to have a Christmas No. 1 with our single but our main priority has always been to raise as much money as we can for good causes.'

Up until now, she had always appeared to be the one who wore the trousers in their relationship but for the first time the single marked a slight change in dynamic with Peter taking the lead as he performed onstage alongside his 'nervous' wife. As well as singing the title track on Children In Need, they also appeared together on the Royal Variety Performance in November 2006 in front of Prince Charles and his wife Camilla. When the royal couple told Peter and Katie at the glamorous televised event they were fans, having 'watched you together in the jungle', it was proof indeed that the singer from Australia and the Page 3 model had, against the odds, captured the heart of an entire nation.

Even better things were to come when a month later Pete's wish came true and Katie announced she was pregnant again. It was great news for the couple, particularly since it came four months after they had revealed the model had suffered a devastating miscarriage. Peter had rushed her to hospital with stomach pains and it was confirmed that she had lost the baby just a few weeks into her pregnancy. Speculation had been mounting that she was expecting again during the album launch and the pair decided to announce the happy news sooner rather than later, realising the stress of keeping it secret might do more damage than good.

Katie told *OK!* magazine: 'I'm due next summer. Because I had the miscarriage I'm saying earlier than I normally would. It's more stressful to keep it secret.'

But far from taking it easy the pair were ploughing ahead with their next task: to conquer America. It had long been Pete's dream to crack the States and they decided to move to Los Angeles for the launch of their new show, *Katie and Peter: The Next Chapter*, which had been picked up by US channel E! It was also being broadcast on ITV2 in the UK, where it received rave reviews and became the station's most-watched programme. That success, however, wasn't to be emulated across the Atlantic and as the couple started a blaze of publicity across America, the show was branded a flop by fierce critics.

'It is the most irrelevant reality show for Americans in the history of irrelevant reality shows. This mess called *Katie & Peter* stars a couple of low rent British celebrities. One is Katie Price, aka Jordan a glamour model, which means she's famous for her double-F implants. The boyfriend of Katie is someone called Peter Andre, a creepy crooner in the order of a modern-day Tom Jones – without cleverness,' said one review.

Many more followed but the couple were determined to make the most of their time out there. For 10 days they rented a beautiful, sprawling mansion in Beverly Hills, along with their now-massive entourage – including Claire their manager, film crew, stylist and make-up team. In between radio and magazine interviews, Peter and heavily pregnant Katie would go sight-seeing or visit attractions like Universal Studios, while in the evenings the loved-up duo would be spotted eating out in some of LA's top eateries.

Some nights they would take it easy and along with the crew, sit down to a huge takeaway around the dining room table.

But the good times were about to come to an abrupt end when it was during one of those slap-up meals that Peter was plunged into the single most frightening experience of his life: out of the blue he was struck down with meningitis. After a fun evening tucking into a giant bucket of Kentucky Fried Chicken, he went to bed and woke up in the middle of the night feeling distinctly odd. 'The chicken kept repeating on me and I could taste the oil, which made me feel very sick – at least that's what I thought was making me feel sick,' he remembered afterwards. 'I also developed a headache at the back of my head. It felt as if something had hit me. However, I managed to get back to bed.'

When Peter woke up the next morning he could barely walk and with Katie and the crew joking he had 'man flu', the singer somehow managed to make it to the airport for their flight home. After being sick eight times mid-flight, he staggered off the plane and despite a doctor visiting him at home and diagnosing flu, the following morning he knew something wasn't right and called 999.

'When he was taken to hospital, he was so weak he had

to be helped on board the ambulance. Katie is obviously frantic with worry,' a friend said at the time.

Doctors at East Surrey Hospital in Redhill carried out a series of emergency tests, including a spinal tap – where a long needle is inserted into the back to take fluid from the spinal cord – and it was then confirmed that Peter had meningitis. To begin with, it wasn't known whether it was bacterial or viral and to that end, whether it could be fatal.

'I was completely motionless and trying to smile through the pain but tears were pouring out of my eyes and at that point I realised things could be serious. I called my parents back home in Australia, but Dad had to get off the phone. He was in tears because the only person he'd known to have meningitis had died.'

There were also fears of Katie contracting the illness, especially being just six weeks away from giving birth to their daughter. Meanwhile there was a rumour going around the internet that Peter had died and 30,000 fans left messages of condolence on his website. The press was going wild with reports he had a 'brain bug'.

'At that stage I didn't know how serious things were. A brain bug sounded terrible and it started to play on my mind. Reports in the papers saying I was dying obviously didn't help either and it was really scary for all of us,' Peter later recalled.

He was finally told he had the less serious strain of viral meningitis and two weeks later – after losing two stone and looking frail and weak – he was discharged from hospital. The doctor's parting shot was: 'Take it easy, Peter – don't do anything for six or seven weeks' but he was determined to get fit and two weeks later the singer was back in the gym. By the following month he had gained his strength back and finally, there was something wonderful to celebrate: the birth of his daughter.

Princess Tiaamii was born on 29 June 2007 at London's Portland Hospital and as with his son Junior, Peter was overjoyed by the birth. Standing outside the hospital he told the waiting press: 'I'm a very happy man now my beautiful wife has given birth to a beautiful baby girl.' Playing the over-protective dad, he joked: 'She's not going out until she is 64. Maybe when she's 30 she can go out with her girlfriends, but that's about it!'

He was revelling in the attention and relieved to at last be standing outside a hospital with good news, rather than for the various traumatic medical emergencies that had befallen his family in the past year. This time too, Katie showed no sign of the postnatal depression that plagued her after Junior's birth and returned home 'over the moon' with their new addition.

It was another month before the couple revealed their daughter's unusual name, during which time it had been rumoured Katie had wanted to call her Crystal after the character in her new novel. The speculators were wrong, of course: they had chosen Princess Tiaamii for two reasons. 'Katie always loved the name Princess. I loved it too but wanted to name her after both our mums. Then I woke up one morning and just knew – we'll put them together – Princess Tiaamii,' he explained to the *Daily Mirror*.

As with their son Junior Savva, Peter was keen to follow the Greek tradition of naming a child after their grandparents

117

and when Katie said she didn't want to use either her mum's name Amy or his mother's Thea, he decided to employ a bit of a poetic licence to get his own way. 'I decided to merge the names together and added a few i's to make it a little more unusual. It suits her perfectly,' he insisted.

Family life now seemed to be back on track and the ever-traditional Mediterranean father was intensely proud of the unmistakeable bond growing between little Princess and his son Junior. Peter had clawed his way back from many crises in his life but finally he had built a close-knit family of his own in the model of the one his parents had lovingly created for him.

'Tiaamii and Junior have a really good brother-sister relationship. It's important you stay close to your siblings – I have always been close to mine so it would be lovely if they stay friends,' he said later. 'You rely on your brothers in both good times and bad times, and if JJ and Tiaamii have a good relationship, it will benefit them.

'I've owned businesses with my siblings, they've played onstage with me when I've been on tour, I've lived with my brother Mike and I just can't imagine not sharing my life with them.'

What Peter didn't realise during those heady post-baby days was that he'd be relying on his family even more for support over the next few months and years.

His relationship with Katie wasn't quite as perfect as it seemed.

CHAPTER EIGHT

WILL THEY, WON'T THEY?

Katie didn't appear to have the postnatal depression she had experienced the first time round, instead she seemed to be on a mission to dive headfirst into a social life again and was on a mission to expand her work empire.

'It'll be a few years before I have another child. Since *I'm A Celebrity*... it seems like I've spent the past three years pregnant. My body is in desperate need of a rest and I'd like to concentrate on my career before number four,' she admitted.

Peter had plenty of projects up his sleeve too, including writing music and investing in property, but to the public at least he was living in the shadow of his fiercely ambitious wife and increasingly seemed to be at home alone looking after the children.

Three weeks after giving birth to Princess, Katie was seen on a five-hour bender across London with good pal and Liberty X star Michelle Heaton. While the star's 'night of shame' ended up with her stumbling out of a nightclub before appearing to be sick out of the back of a car, Peter was back at their mansion dutifully babysitting their brood.

Fans of the singer were aghast at the way his wife was treating him. One fan wrote to the *Sun* newspaper: 'Katie Price doesn't deserve such a wonderful husband as Peter Andre. She was out drinking with pals just a few weeks after having daughter Princess Tiaamii, who will be made fun of, thanks to that awful name.'

Katie's nights out became more frequent and she was overheard moaning that the reason she wasn't in the papers anymore was because no one was interested in a new mum. While Peter was always quick to fob off serious claims their marriage was a ticking time bomb, he himself had started to hint that he wasn't entirely happy and their sex life was suffering again.

'I think she's got post-husband depression – she's not giving me any love at all!' he lamented to the cameras in their ITV2 reality show.

But when Katie was spotted on a night out with friends without her wedding ring while Peter was in Cyprus, rumours started to circulate that their marriage was seriously on the rocks this time. Quick to dismiss them and defend his wife, Peter told the *Daily Star*: 'These stories saying Jordan is taking her wedding ring off because our relationship is in trouble hurt. Because Kate has been out having a great time with her pals while I'm here in Cyprus, people have jumped to the wrong conclusions. She's just doing what anyone would be doing right now after all she's been through recently. The simple truth is I'm out here getting things ready for my family to come out and visit – including the children.'

But the couple's fans might have been forgiven for making wrong assumptions, not only was Peter claiming to be sex-starved, Katie added fuel to the fire by saying she slept in a body bag. She joked to *OK!* magazine: 'I'm using St Tropez tan now – I put it on at night, then zip myself into a body suit so it doesn't get on the sheets. Only my feet and face are out, so we have to have bedroom activities on other nights.'

Although the claim was tongue-in-cheek, the couple's public bickering continued and messages about their ailing sex life were becoming increasingly mixed with Katie, in particular, sometimes doing a complete U-turn in claiming the chemistry between them was the best it had ever been.

With her new perfume, Stunning, to promote and feeling 'more ambitious than ever', Peter's wife boasted at its launch that the scent drove him wild.

'Peter loves it,' she announced, 'In fact when I wear it he can't keep his hands off me! I'm sure when women wear it, it will turn men on – it's a great pulling perfume.'

Although they still had plenty of joint career plans in the footing, including a talk show and a fresh assault on America, the same couldn't be said of some aspects of their social life.

Katie had always loved horse riding and with her own stables at home, she was devoting more and more time to hanging out with the horsey set. She was now writing pony novels for children and had been spotted at Royal Ascot – a clear indication she was moving in new social circles which Peter couldn't really be part of. But while it looked on the surface as if Katie was selfishly hogging the limelight at her husband's expense, Peter was actually harbouring some deep-seated problems that were preventing him from enjoying life as his wife seemed to be.

The panic attacks had started up again and his fear of public spaces, particularly nightclubs, had returned. He had felt a resurgence of the disorder following his meningitis scare and doctors believed the terrifying illness coupled with his fear of dying during the episode had triggered post-traumatic stress disorder. He had also been left shaken after his stepson Harvey was rushed to hospital with burn injuries after scalding himself in the bath shortly after Katie announced she was pregnant with their daughter.

'Since having the meningitis and since Harvey's recent accident it's brought back the panic attacks which I hadn't had for nearly two years. So I decided to go and see one of the best therapists and address a few issues,' he admitted on his ITV2 show. 'There are some things I've been meaning to talk about for a while and as I've not been talking about them they've been getting more and more out of control. For example, I have a problem with drink – I don't need to stop drinking, I need to find a way to start drinking. I won't go anywhere that is alcohol based.'

It was clear that while Katie had been keen to regain her social life after giving birth, Peter's mental health issues were holding him back. He had also become reliant on anti-depressants and wanted to start taking control again.

'The other problem is that I've been on medication for a few years now, but it's such a minimal dose that I'm scared to come off that. Occasionally I do want to go out – we are young, you know? I know in my heart of hearts I don't need to be on this medication but I need to get help,' he added.

Although he was taking steps to get better, it wasn't going to happen overnight and already it was clearly driving a wedge between him and Katie. But it wasn't all doom and gloom for the most talked-about husband and wife team for when it came to their careers Peter and Katie were still a united front. Firstly they announced they were planning to launch themselves in America, where they wanted to find fame with a new reality TV show.

Peter seemed to be a lot more laid-back about the plans with a more 'let's see what happens' attitude, while Katie appeared desperate to make it big.

'I'm going to be knocking Posh Spice off every magazine rack in the country. Once they've got a load of us, they won't be interested in the Beckhams,' she said at the time.

Then in November 2007, their late night chat show *Katie and Peter: Unleashed* was launched on ITV2, which featured celebrity guests, music, audience games and behind-the-scenes footage. With their on-screen banter, petty squabbles and a host of celebrity guests including Boy George, Nicole Scherzinger and Rupert Everett, the short-lived show pulled in over a million viewers at its peak.

One review at the time said: 'Unless you're tuning in to this show from an anthropological point of view (as I do) then this is certainly enthralling television for the intellectually challenged. This is not just "trash TV"', this is trashy "trash TV" with a perma-tan glow.'

In a whirlwind of money making projects, Katie had also applied to register her real name Katie Price as a trademark. The mum-of-three wanted to use the name to endorse a range of hair products, bed linen and make-up to add to her already bulging CV.

There was simply no comparison between Peter's career and his wife's but far from being hidden in the shadows, the singer was still very much in the celebrity spotlight as the fourth series of their reality show, *Katie and Peter: The Next Chapter*, was broadcast to the nation in early 2008. By now, the couple had amassed a fortune of over £30million and there was still plenty of mileage in their marriage yet if their 1.25 million viewers had anything to do with it.

In a bid to delight their fans, the pair were seen on their TV show returning to the Australian bush where they had first met on *I'm A Celebrity...* to share their first jungle kiss, which they hadn't braved for the cameras the first time round. It also served as a reminder to the public of how much they had achieved together since starring and falling in love on the hit ITV1 show.

'We were in Australia visiting Pete's family and we asked if we could go back to the camp and have a look at it again for our show. We're the only people ever to be allowed back in,' Katie told the *Sun*.

'It was so weird crossing that bridge again. We were standing there in the camp, which looks just the same, and we suddenly thought, "Ah, we can have a kiss now." We couldn't do that at the time because we didn't want to be snogging on camera. It was so long ago and so much seems to have happened since then. Not many couples stay together for four years in the showbiz world so it was nice to go back and remember how it all started.'

In a further sign of unity Peter was treated to a romantic dinner at a top fish restaurant for his 35th birthday in February by his wife.

The duo continued to look like the adoring couple when Peter admitted in an interview to promote their new series that he still wanted a large family with Katie and they loved staying in watching real-life crime shows together. 'We love Forensic Detectives. That's one of our faves,' he revealed. 'We are not The Osbournes. We are The Andreborns. For some reason people want to watch us. I think they like seeing the whole family. It's not just about Katie and I. We want at least six or seven kids so there's plenty more to see from us.'

Peter also supported his wife's now obsession with riding and all-things equestrian – even giving Katie another horse called Dana for her 30th birthday in May. Her interest in the sport had now cranked up a gear and as well as eventing – including taking part in the revered Horse of the Year Show – she was taking daily dressage lessons from renowned trainer Andrew Gould. Although little was made of it at the time, Katie's life was now so taken up with riding, with dreams of competing in the Olympics, it was difficult to see where Peter fitted in. But it didn't seem to bother him. Instead, the singer appeared to publicly support his wife's new love affair and when she was humiliated after being refused VIP entry at the Cartier International Polo contest in Windsor, he was the first to voice outrage on her behalf.

'I'm protective. It's upsetting because Katie's really got her heart set on horses,' he said at the time. 'It's the one thing I know she's more passionate about than anything – as a hobby, as a first love.'

When their chat show was axed in the autumn of 2008, neither Peter nor Katie seemed particularly upset since they already had another reality TV series in the pipeline. This time their captive audience would be privy to the pair renewing their wedding vows in a romantic, low-key ceremony in South Africa.

'It was a mind-blowing trip, filled with all sorts of activities and I loved it. We were there to renew our vows, something that Kate really wanted.

'If I'm honest, after just three years of marriage I thought it was too early but she really wanted to do it and said the main reason was so that she could change her surname to Andre afterwards,' Peter said in later years.

Although the name change never happened, it was obvious that despite their public bickering and rumours all was not well behind the scenes, they clearly still wanted to make a go of it. After all, Peter had always maintained that due to his religious upbringing and Greek family traditions he would do everything to stay married and provide crucial stability for his much-loved children.

The 'love affirmation ceremony' was also an opportunity to set the record straight and prove to the world that they were still in love.

Speaking at the exclusive Thornybush Game Reserve in Kruger National Park where the couple took their vows, Katie told *OK!* magazine: 'We are not breaking up. We're in love, for God's sake. It's never got that bad. We have big fights but I've never thought it's over – and neither has Pete.

'There's nothing that would make us break up – unless one of us was unfaithful. The only thing that would make him walk out on me is if I cheated on him, and that's never going to happen, so he's never going to walk out on me. I love him to bits.'

Sadly it did little to quieten the sceptics.

Peter was again at the centre of split rumours when two months after the intimate ceremony, he jetted to Los Angeles with his brothers on a 'boys' break' to work on the re-launch of his music career. Looking lonely and miserable he had been spotted dining on his own while Kate was back home launching a new range of haircare products.

Back in the UK rumours were rife that Katie, who had been spotted on several occasions again without her engagement ring, was fed up with Peter's lack of work, leaving her to support the family. A family friend also claimed they were on the verge of a break-up after Katie had flown into a jealous rage over his nineties affair with Spice Girl Mel B – accusing him of still holding a torch for her. Not only that, the couple seemed to have begun to lead separate lives after they were spotted at two different nightclubs in London on the same night.

A friend told the *Sunday Mirror*: 'The most time they ever spend together is when they are on the TV show. When the cameras are off, it's a different story. Peter is a real family man who loves being with the kids and cooking for the family. He likes days out as a family and dinners together around the table. But Katie has let him down loads of times when he has been expecting her home and has prepared a meal. She is often working or off horse-riding. There have been lots of rows.'

Despite Peter dismissing it as a 'load of b******s', when Katie jetted out to Los Angeles to meet him, the couple put on an unconvincing show of togetherness. After going for dinner at a tapas restaurant they emerged half an hour later hand-in-hand but looking far from happy.

What Peter probably didn't realise at the time was that courtesy of their reality TV show the public had been witnessing the breakdown of a marriage for some time now. There were the endless squabbles, the moaning about their ailing sex life and in one telling scene Peter looked close to breaking point. It wasn't anything new, mind you – just one of many rows which had started to make the show exhausting viewing throughout 2008 but the scene was so desperate it felt as though the end wasn't far away.

In an argument on Katie's birthday, Peter turned to his wife as he dropped her off at a beauty salon and said: 'You've made me feel like shit again, on your birthday this time. I didn't think that could possibly happen.

'But that's alright. What you do is make everyone feel the same way you do. If you don't like yourself, you make everyone else feel like shit and that's unfair.'

When she'd left the car, Peter told the camera: 'Honestly, she is so hard to live with, she is such hard work. I've never had so much stress as I've had trying to live with that woman, she treats everyone like shit, I'm f*****g sick of it!'

In fact he was so fed up that unbeknownst to the outside world, 11 months before their split, he had insisted on a trial separation. Peter went to Cyprus for ten days, while Katie stayed at home and in a make-or-break deal, they both underwent marriage counselling.

'I felt she didn't love me anymore but I was still determined to try to salvage things, make it work for us and for the kids,' he finally confessed to the *News Of The World* a year after their split. 'We both had counselling. There were four things we both agreed to change and within two weeks, I had changed every single one. Kate didn't bother.'

To the outside world the strains were obviously growing day by day but as the New Year approached, their fans were still hanging on and so were they, by all accounts.

'This year has been great,' Katie insisted adamantly. 'Pete and I are getting on the best we ever have. I know we bicker a lot and wind each other up but that's just the way we are. The other night we were watching re-runs of *I'm A Celebrity*... Even then we were picking on each other.

'He's my lover and my best friend. I get on with his family and he gets on with mine. I know he's always complaining that he never gets enough sex, but when he does get it, it's the best quality!'

When the couple guest-edited the *Daily Mirror*'s '3am' showbiz column soon afterwards, Katie revealed she was trying hard to set aside her jealous tendencies and even planning to meet up with Peter's ex, Mel B.

'I get so jealous,' she wrote, 'but it's getting better now I'm getting older.

'I'm even supposed to be meeting up with Mel B, Pete's ex, in LA.

'We've been texting each other about getting together

and considering Pete used to be obsessed with her, that's quite a big step forward for me.'

In February 2009 it was time to conquer America and Peter flew his family to Los Angeles to live there for three months. It was to be something of a 'fresh start' with the singer hungry to write music out there and the pair now desperate to get away from the mayhem of the UK and try something new. The adventure would also be captured for their latest reality TV show, *Katie and Peter: Stateside*.

Based in Malibu, the couple rented out a stunning £70,000-a-month, eight-bedroom Mediterranean-style villa in an exclusive gated community. As well as an outdoor pool, it also boasted a gym, music editing suite cinema and games room, and had Britney Spears and Barbra Streisand for neighbours.

The three children, six-year-old Harvey, Junior, three, and 20-month Princess Tiaamii, quickly took to LA's good-weather outdoor lifestyle, which reminded Peter of the idyllic childhood days he had spent with his own father, growing up on Australia's Gold Coast.

While Katie enjoyed horse riding at their new home's private stables, Peter started work on his new album straight away. Working in a studio owned by actor Will Smith, he teamed up with a host of big-name producers for the new record.

'Everyone in the industry is expecting it to be rubbish,' he admitted. 'That's what's driving me because I know what I'm capable of and I know what I've released before. I know there have been some shockers, I'm going to be the first to admit it, but there's no excuse.'

His gritty determination was to pay off. When *Revelation* was released later that year it went platinum after peaking at No. 3 n the charts.

Back in America, Peter was also focused on a massive fitness drive after he and Katie had decided to run the London Marathon on their return to Britain in April. The sprint was a chance for them to achieve something together with a bid to raise £280,000 for the two charities, NSPCC and Vision. Photos streaming back to the UK were often of the pair taking early morning sunrise runs along the beach as they tried to lose weight and get fit for what would turn out to be their last ever public venture together.

'I love it over here and have really been able to knuckle down and get on with the album,' Peter told the *Daily Mirror*. 'Running along the beach and seeing dolphins diving in and out of the waves is also a bit different to wrapping up in sub-zero conditions and running against the wind along Brighton Pier! I've lost over a stone and a half in weight since I started training and want to get really ripped by the day of the marathon.

'We're both still eating absolute c**p though so we're seeing a specialist nutritionist who's taking our body fat percentages and giving us an eating plan.'

'It's so easy to be fit and look after yourself properly out here. I love it,' Katie gushed. Clearly taken with Los Angeles, she added: 'I popped into Paris Hilton's birthday party, two weeks ago. I met her a couple of years ago at the World Music Awards and we've stayed in touch. She's great. On the night of her party, I wasn't drinking because of the

PETER ANDRE – THE BIOGRAPHY

running so I didn't stay long. It was at her Beverly Hills home, which was pretty impressive. It was an amazing bash.

'We chatted with Gordon Ramsay and his wife Tana at Elton John's post-Oscar party. They're a really fun couple. I like them because they banter with each other and have a laugh, like Pete and I do. Mel B's also out in LA and is super fit. She's great, so we may well catch up with her soon.

'The house we're renting has stables and a paddock so I'm able to go riding every morning if I want to. It's brilliant. Although Victoria Beckham and I have had our problems, Pete said "hello" to her at Elton John's Oscar bash and they got on great. All in all, the lifestyle over here is brilliant.'

But the truth of the matter was, Katie wasn't happy at all and was finding it extremely hard to adapt. The main problem appeared to be that the couple were having something of a role reversal.

While Peter was pursuing his lifelong dream of recording music in the States, Katie was really only there to film the show. She wasn't working as she did back in Britain but was either at home or out shopping.

'Until this point it was me who was used to being in the shadow – yes, I never stopped writing music but I wasn't recording or in the limelight in the same way as Katie. Now for the first time the boot was on the other foot. I wanted so much for her to be a part of it all. So many times I asked her to come down to the studio but she just wouldn't.

'The cracks were really beginning to show to the outside world; the press were picking up on our row in the show which had moved up a gear, and there seemed to be leaks everywhere – it wasn't nice for either of us,' Peter remembered, years later.

In fact, their time in America, just a month before their split, marked the lowest point in Peter's relationship with Katie. A comment the singer made after taking a break in recording to speak to the cameras filming their ITV2 show said it all: 'I love her incredibly but when I hate her, I hate her. Hate's a bad word – when I'm not happy, I'm very not happy.'

Back in Britain and with the London Marathon just around the corner, Peter was doing his best to put on a brave face and look to the future.

'We've been absolutely knackered for the past few weeks so there are two main reasons I want to complete the run: one, because it's for charity and two, because we can get back to normal action in the bedroom.

'Kate's promised it'll happen on Sunday night but I'm guessing she'll be pretty knackered after all that running. Even if she's not, I might not be fit for it! But thank God our sex life should be back on track pretty soon – I can't wait.'

Sadly it wasn't to be. Although the pair made it over the finishing line in a respectable 7 hours and 11 minutes, it was to be their last public display of unity. Their three-and-a-half year marriage had run its distance and had irretrievably broken down.

In a final blow, Katie was snapped cosying up to a man at a party on a night out with her horsey pals just days after she and Peter had completed the Marathon together. He was said to have 'exploded' after seeing the photos of his wife canoodling with a stranger in a Bristol nightclub following the Badminton Horse Trials.

Although the man at the centre of the allegations later claimed to be gay, Katie's dressage coach Andrew Gould was also snapped at the party and Peter had long been concerned there was something going on between them.

A source said at the time: 'Peter had become convinced Katie preferred spending time at the paddock and with her horse-riding pals. He flew into a jealous rage when he saw the photos of her horseplay at the club in Bristol. It was the final straw.'

True, it had been a catalyst, but Peter's decision to split from his wife came as no surprise to anyone – except, perhaps, the woman who he had once vowed to spend the rest of his life with. For Peter his mind was made up while on their bittersweet family holiday in Los Angeles when their fragile relationship had become something of a ticking time bomb. He had tried marriage counselling, a trial separation even, but in truth it had all been too little, too late.

'The L.A. trip was a busy time,' he admitted after their divorce. 'I was living on adrenalin and loving writing music but it signalled the lowest point for my relationship with Katie.

'I don't think it was a huge surprise to anyone when we finally announced our separation on that fateful day, 11 May 2009.'

CHAPTER NINE

GOING IT ALONE

The nation seemed in a state of shock. Despite the years of rows and public sniping, Peter and Katie's announcement seemed to come like a bolt from the blue:

Peter Andre and Katie Price are separating after four and a half years of marriage. They have both requested that the media respect their families' privacy at this difficult time.

The public couldn't quite believe how quickly the situation had worsened and they wanted answers. Was it a publicity stunt? Who was to blame? What would happen to the children?

Just three days before the split, Peter had put on a united front with his wife leaving a top London restaurant hand-in-hand after filming a piece for the British Soap Awards. Now there seemed to be little chance of the nation's sweethearts reconciling.

Peter had made it clear his decision was final and on leaving the family home he fled to his manager Claire's house, where he stayed until he had time to sort himself out. Bizarrely, in the days following, he realised that telling Katie it was over had been the easy part, confessing to his deeply religious parents that he was going to divorce was incredibly tough.

'I wanted to have what my parents have: a marriage that lasted forever. The hardest thing for me about my split was not walking away from Kate but picking up the phone to tell my parents. I felt like I'd failed. I'd been brought up as a Jehovah's Witness that didn't acknowledge divorce unless for extreme reasons,' he said.

Even though it went against everything he believed in, Peter was adamant he wasn't going to go back and after jetting to his Cyprus hideaway he spent a week with his ever-supportive family coming to terms with his new single status. Katie, meanwhile, had fled to the luxury Maldives villa they had honeymooned in with their two children, Junior and Princess.

Peter was devastated. He had walked out on Katie, not the children, but it felt like the family unit he'd so proudly nurtured had been completely obliterated.

On his return to Britain, the singer found a house in Hove, West Sussex, forty miles from the family home, and as he set about trying to make it as nice as possible for Harvey, Junior and Princess, the reality of what had happened came crashing down. While Peter didn't regret his decision in breaking up with Katie, he certainly hadn't bargained on the sheer pain of being separated from their children.

'In the first few days all I could think about were my kids. I knew I had to be strong for them, so I went to Ikea to buy furniture, duvets and pillowcases to go in the new home I'd bought for them. It was at that point it really hit me hard – the realisation that the family unit was smashed to pieces. I got out of the shop and sat in the car with my brother Mike and just broke down.

'It wasn't about Katie – it was about us being a mum and dad to our kids. I was buying all these things to create a second home and I was telling Junior, Princess and Harvey how lucky they were to have two houses now, but inside it was killing me. I literally broke down and cried myself to sleep.'

Peter was finding it hard, but things were to get a whole lot worse before they got better as the relationship with his ex immediately turned nasty. Katie swung from saying she wanted Pete back to lashing out at him, both publicly and in private phone calls, and while he was trying hard to keep a dignified silence it was proving impossible. As ever their relationship was being played out in public and in a bid to set straight scores of rumours, including claims he had cheated on her, he would often end up giving his side of the story.

She accused him of being jealous and controlling, to which he replied, 'No one can control Katie, find anyone who can and I'll shake them by the hand.'

There were also the cynics who made out that it was a ploy on Peter's part to inherit a fortune from his wife, that he'd had an affair or the whole fiasco was a publicity stunt.

'I insisted on a pre-nup,' he retaliated in a newspaper

over rumours he'd only married for money. 'Katie didn't want one. We had a huge row about it because she thought it meant I wanted a divorce. I told her it was because I never wanted her to think I was after her money. I paid half of everything while we were married – holidays, furniture, cars...'

Trying to put to rest the infidelity rumours, he added: 'She's the only woman I've been with since we got together. I'd take a lie-detector test to prove that.'

The question of custody was also now playing heavy on his mind and with Katie clearly in a fragile state he had every reason to worry. His worst fears were confirmed when in the wake of their separation Peter asked if he could take her disabled son Harvey to Cyprus while she was in the Maldives with their other two children.

She refused – and in a cruel twist, she chose to leave him in the care of his father, Dwight Yorke, who had rarely been there for his son, along with a nanny and her mum Amy. A friend said: 'Peter asked to fly Harvey out to Cyprus with him and had flights provisionally booked. First, he was told Harvey wasn't allowed any more days off from his special school. But even when Pete suggested flying him over to Cyprus this weekend, the answer was still "No".

'Kate told him she wanted Harvey to be with her mother and not him. He is absolutely gutted. The pair had several furious phone calls and some pretty hostile things were said.

'For the past five years, Pete has brought Harvey up as his own flesh and blood. He loves the boy as much as he

Peter Andre hits the red carpet for The Pride of Britain Awards in 2011

Above Left: A youthful Peter promoting one of his earlier singles back in 1995.

Above Right: Younger years: showing off a striking physique and an even more striking haircut…

Below: Before entering the jungle to take part in *I'm a Celebrity… Get Me Out of Here!* in 2004.

Above Left: Better days: Peter with his ex-wife Katie Price at the *I'm a Celebrity…* reunion.   © *Rex Features*

Above right: He must take after his daddy! Doting Peter and his son, Junior, both wearing hats at the *Ice Age 2* premiere.   © *Rex Features*

Below: A Royal meeting! Peter and Katie shake hands with Prince Charles after the Royal Variety Performance in 2006.   © *Rex Features*

Above Left: Peter with his award for Celebrity Dad of the Year in 2010.

Above Right: Peter spends some precious family time with his mum, and children.

Below: Definitely a daddy's girl! Peter cuddles up to his gorgeous daughter
Princess Tiaamii.

Top: Not just a pretty face: Peter launches his first coffee shop in East Grinstead, West Sussex.© *Rex Features*

Bottom: Mayor of London, Boris Johnson, and Peter Andre launching their reading and literacy project for children in the summer of 2011. © *Rex Features*

Above left: Seeing double: Peter unveils his own Waxwork at Louis Tussauds Waxworks
© Rex Feature

Above right: Peter rocking the stage during his concert at the 02 Academy in Oxford.
© Rex Feature

Below: Peter gives back at the launch of the BBC Children in Need POP Goes the Musical with fellow stars the Sugababes and Stacey Solomon.
© Rex Feature

Above left: Peter Andre hitting the red carpet with his brothers Chris and Danny.

© *Rex Features*

Above right: All in white: Peter looks suave as he promotes his new TV programme *The Next Chapter*.

© *Rex Features*

Below left: Spending quality time with his son Junior outside the ITV studios.

© *Rex Features*

Below right: Looking glamorous as he hits the red carpet with his current girlfriend Emily Macdonagh at the National Television awards.

© *Rex Features*

Peter picks up his award for Digital TV Personality at the TRIC TV and
Radio awards.

does his own biological children and the fact Kate has Junior and Princess with her at the moment is killing him.'

For Peter, the enormity of what was happening and the break-up of his treasured family saw him spiral into a depression, so much so that he hid himself away whenever possible and was struggling to eat.

'When we split up, I couldn't even look at myself in the mirror and I locked myself in my manager's house. All my confidence vanished and I felt so anxious and stressed out that my appetite disappeared and I could barely eat,' he later confessed.

Matters weren't helped by the public's incessant questions over why he had finally thrown in the towel after it was rumoured Peter had twice consulted divorce lawyers in the past year.

While he was adamant he had never been unfaithful, the reasons he gave for dumping his wife seemed to indicate something untoward had happened. It was true to say no one could believe the couple would consider divorce unless someone else was involved since both Peter and Katie had maintained at one time or another that only infidelity would tear them apart.

One man, Katie's horse trainer Andrew Gould, stood squarely in the frame as being the 'other man' who ultimately forced the collapse of the marriage. A photo in a newspaper of Katie out drinking with the handsome dad-of-two on a wild night out in a Bristol nightclub with their horsey pals was thought to be the final nail in the coffin of their doomed marriage. Peter was said to be incensed, particularly since handsome Andrew initially denied he was at the party.

Within days of the split the married riding instructor spoke out to defend himself. Claiming their relationship was completely innocent, he also admitted he had only lied because Katie was worried it would wind up her husband.

'I'm not interested in Kate at all in that way. I did initially say I wasn't the guy in the club because Kate didn't want Peter to know,' he explained to the *Sun* newspaper. 'It is so innocent and so ridiculous. The whole evening ended at half two. I went to a friend's house and Katie went back to her hotel. My wife was out too.'

His wife Polly, who also looked after Katie's four horses, waded into the argument, saying the former Page 3 girl would never destroy their marriage.

But while Peter never actually accused his wife of having an affair, he didn't mind admitting he believed Katie was obsessed with the 29-year-old horseman and it had put a massive strain on their marriage. 'I would never ask her to stop riding but I did ask her to move her horses or get a new instructor. She didn't. It was no secret among our friends I was unhappy,' he said in an interview, a year later. 'When we weren't working I always wanted us to have a family day with the kids. I'd wake up and she'd have left already to go riding. In America she'd go out riding with no make-up but here she'd go out on her horse fully made up.

'Let me make it clear I was totally faithful to her. I never so much as held another girl's hand during our marriage. The vows we took meant everything to me.'

But Katie was quick to tackle the story head on, claiming it was all in Pete's imagination and he was simply being a jealous husband. 'Pete had it in his head that I fancied him, he fancied me. Every time I'd go to the horse I'd come back in a good mood and Pete would look at me as if Andrew's making me in a good mood. So it grew in his head until he ended up thinking something was going on. I told him, "There's nothing going on." But by then it was too late.'

To this day, Peter has never given a definitive reason for their split, saying he wants to wait until his children are old enough to explain it to them first. But roundabout answers always hinted that he had good reason, which has kept his fans guessing ever since.

'There have been times when I've been dying to tell the world what really happened but then I think of my dad, who has counselled me to say nothing, and think of the damage it would do to the children,' he once offered up as an explanation. Another time he simply stated: 'Katie knows why, ask her.'

But in a candid interview with TV host Piers Morgan, Peter confirmed there was a big secret behind their split – and it wasn't necessarily the cheating rumours everyone believed it to be.

'Katie said the reason I left her was because I'd seen pictures of her in nightclubs flirting with other men and presumed she'd cheated on me. That is not the truth. Those pictures were not the reason I left Katie. I would never end a marriage over something small, or little things building up.

'Something big happened, which I won't reveal as I don't want my kids reading it. But when I tell them, I'll come on your show and reveal what actually happened. Katie knows 100 per cent the reason why I left her and I am 100 per cent sure that what happened definitely did happen.'

While Peter was still shaken by the ordeal, he seemed at least to gain strength from seeing his children at weekends and hanging out with his brothers after he handed them back to his ex. After being photographed in the early days of their separation playing with Junior and Princess on Brighton beach, he admitted: 'It's been tough but being with them is the best tonic in the world. I missed them so much when they were away from me – it was the worst part of what has happened.'

Katie, meanwhile, wasn't handling the split well. With her usual bravado the former glamour model seemed to deal with the crisis head on by clubbing, drinking and flirting with men. While at times she was visibly heartbroken, her temper sometimes got the better of her and in one vicious swipe she wrote on her Twitter page: 'Peter's being a true c**t to me. He left me, not me leave him. I want a drink. I want to get off my nut. Let's go to the bar and get on with it.'

Peter may have been the one to call time on their relationship and the most likely to be in the public's firing line but Katie's out-of-control antics were doing her no favours. She was quickly losing public sympathy and while she had always been as popular as her husband, the public were now seeing them as two different characters: wild Katie and saintly Pete. And much to his surprise, the Peter camp was clearly winning.

'Katie's hit rock bottom,' a friend said, 'She doesn't know what to do with herself. She's been sobbing, calling Peter and attacking anyone she can.

'Her friends are worried she's drinking too much.'

Peter was now veering between anger and concern but when she jetted to Ibiza for a week-long booze fest, during which she was snapped cavorting drunkenly with male models and flashing her underwear, his sympathy turned to outrage. She also hooked up with 28-year-old model Anthony Lowther during the holiday and photos of her wild antics back in Britain seemed to be getting worse by the day.

'It's like a wild animal has been unleashed,' Peter told a friend – who in stark contrast was playing dutiful dad on holiday with their children in Cyprus. 'I don't recognise her as my wife. Has she no idea what this will be like for the kids? It was Katie who I fell in love with and married but it looks like she just wanted all along to be her old self, Jordan. I can't believe what I'm seeing.'

It didn't help that the day after touching down in Britain she went for a private riding session with Andrew Gould at his West Sussex stables before going to the pub. In a dramatic showdown, Peter called her up to tell her how much he disapproved.

'I did phone her to tell her she was a disgrace. I said that because that was what I thought. Of course it gets to me and if any other man was in my position I'm sure they would feel pretty bad,' he declared.

The pair were both knocked for six by the split and although dealing with it in completely different ways, it was visibly taking its toll and they were losing a worrying amount of weight.

Three months into his split, the singer had shed three stone and couldn't eat. 'I had this horrible twisted knot of anxiety and hurt inside my stomach. I was losing weight by the day but I still couldn't eat. I felt so bad, I just couldn't swallow food – I went from 13st 8lb to 10st12lb,' he revealed.

Luckily for Peter his family was rallying round to help him come to terms with his new life. His sister Debbie had flown all the way from Australia to Cyprus to offer moral support and in a bid to cheer him up, his mum Thea had decided to surprise her son by making the trip too.

On seeing his mother at the airport, Peter broke down. It was another reminder of the important role his family played in his life, especially during a crisis.

'He had no idea his mum was coming so when he went to collect his sister from the airport and saw Thea it was all too much,' a friend revealed. 'The emotion of the past six weeks caught up with him and as much as he wanted to hold it together, he couldn't. Thea will give him some much-needed TLC and wants to look after him as only a mother can.'

In a bizarre way, as difficult as it may have been to see his wife drunkenly making out with other men, it was clearly making it easier for Peter to move on, too.

'I've shed my last tear for her. Kate is right about one thing: there were three of us in our marriage – me, Kate and Jordan,' he told his cousin Angelo.

Fortunately, Peter still had work to keep him focused and thanks to his three months recording in LA in the run-up to the split, there was plenty to distract him from his messy home life. Not only that, on a trip to Macau in China to perform at the Indian Film Academy

Awards in June 2009, he was given a standing ovation in rehearsals and it gave him just the confidence boost he needed.

'The response I've had since being in China has been absolutely amazing,' he said. 'I never expected the attention I've been getting and I am so glad this is happening. This and the work I'm doing now is beginning to give me confidence again. Singing has given me something to focus on. Finally, I'm beginning to smile again.'

Of course there were still moments of sadness as he tried to come to terms with his impending divorce. One night he completely broke down while enjoying a meal out in China with his manager Claire and brother Michael. Peter had to be shielded from view by the pair as grief for what he had lost completely washed over him and he started sobbing uncontrollably.

'I just lost it. I got hit by this sudden feeling of loss and I just broke down. I wish I was stronger. The one thing about Katie is that she can just move on. I can't do that. Well, not yet anyway,' he confessed at the time.

Taking the heartbreaking decision to walk away from his marriage had required Peter to draw on his last reserves of strength and he realised that yet again he was faced with the arduous task of building his life up again. It was another enforced fresh start for the singer but this time at least he had more fans than ever and with years of experience behind him, he knew the only way to turn things around was to get fit, eat well, spend quality time with his children and focus on his music and TV work.

His manager Claire Powell of CAN Associates had

chosen to stick by Pete over Katie after working with him for 15 years and together they put a plan into action.

'For three months people have seen me crying and hurt, and going through all that. I was suffering – down one minute and happy the next. But whatever happens can't hurt me anymore,' he told the *Daily Mirror* newspaper. 'Of course it's sad – it's the break-up of a marriage. But I've finally turned the corner and I'm ready to move on with my life.'

In another interview, he added: 'I lost myself in my marriage. I lost my confidence and I'm slowly beginning to build it back up again.

'After the split I'd have given myself two out of 10 – that's how low I'd got. I want to focus on getting healthy again, eating properly, being with my kids. I'd like people to listen to me with fresh ears. As a musician I want to be given another chance.'

And his wish was granted. Just three months after the split Peter had plenty to celebrate. Firstly, his new reality show, *Peter Andre: Going It Alone*, was broadcast on ITV2. In a surreal twist when the couple split, their TV show split too and Katie had her own fly-on-the-wall series *What Katie Did Next* to rival his on ITV. Since the cameras had been there to document every intimate detail of the split and the heartbreaking weeks that followed, there was plenty of juicy material for Peter's gossip-hungry fans.

Following a £1million deal with independent record label Conehead, the singer was also knee-deep in promoting his first solo album in five years, *Revelation*. The comeback single, 'Behind Closed Doors', taken off the record was released in August, a month before the album, and it surpassed all expectations in peaking at No. 4.

As its title suggests, the song was written about his relationship with Katie and with it hitting the shops just three short months after their acrimonious separation, it couldn't have received better publicity.

In another single from the album, 'Call The Doctor', there was an even clearer indication that Peter was spilling the beans on their bitter break-up through his music, although Peter later explained that he had never intended it to be a statement to the public, more that the album had been like 'therapy' for him. But Katie saw it as another opportunity to take a swipe at her husband and claimed it was proof he had ended the marriage to sell his music.

'If it's all about me and him not getting on, how would he be promoting his album if he was still happily married to me?' she asked. 'It feels like he was maybe waiting for an excuse to end it. He's not the same Pete I knew.'

Indeed Peter had changed, but not necessarily in the way Katie was referring to. The album heralded a new musical direction for the singer and in his first big interview since the split, he admitted to Radio 1 DJ Chris Moyles that he was deeply proud of his work.

Recorded while out in LA with a host of big name artists, including Coolio and Montell Jordan, the songs were more centred on the lyrics than the catchy melodies his previous records had been renowned for.

In simple terms: it came from the heart.

Describing the album as 'urban rock', he told Moyles: 'It couldn't be more on the other side of the world from

Insania. I should have done an album like this years ago. I just thought the stuff people write in their diaries, why not write it in a song?

'It's the first time I've been given the chance to lyrically do something. I know I've got a lot to prove in this country and I totally understand why.'

But he had nothing to worry about for the album was a massive success and stormed the charts, by reaching No. 3 and going platinum after shifting 300,000 copies. Peter Mania had taken hold again.

He had now signed deals worth £3.5million, including his own fragrance *Unconditional*, a slot as a reporter on ITV breakfast show *This Morning*, his own reality TV show and was the face of Christian Audigier's Ed Hardy clothing range, previously modelled by Madonna and Michael Jackson. Peter was starting to get mobbed again by fans and several album signings had to be cancelled after tens of thousands of people turned up, blocking motorways and making the events a logistical nightmare.

'I'd be at a signing that was supposed to last two hours and I ended up staying seven or eight to meet as many people as I could! A lot had to be cancelled because there wasn't enough security to deal with it,' he said.

At the launch of his album *Revelation* in one ASDA store, ambulance crews had to treat 12 girls after they fainted as Peter turned up in a blacked-out car complete with police escort.

Over 9,000 fans had stormed the supermarket, with scores climbing up on shelves and into shopping trolleys to catch a glimpse of their chart-topping hero arriving to sign copies of his record. At one point, Peter had to be led away to safety as a mob broke through the barriers to get closer to him.

One fan said at the time: 'It was like Beatlemania. I have never seen anything like this. People were going crazy.'

Letters in their thousands and even food parcels from fans were flooding into his management's office. And it wasn't just the public showing their support, a host of celebrities were coming out of the woodwork to rally round him too. Footballer Frank Lampard made a detour to meet him at a Beyoncé gig, while Vinnie Jones, Michael Jackson's brother Tito and TV presenter Fiona Phillips all admitted to being on 'Team Peter'. When he presented an award at the O2 Silver Clef Awards in London in aid of the Nordoff-Robbins music therapy charity, Denise Van Outen introduced him to the star-studded audience, which included Gary Barlow, Queen, the Stereophonics, Lulu and Madness, by saying: 'Who's on Team Andre then?'

As he took to the stage to present N-Dubz with the Best Digital award, Peter was given a standing ovation by everyone in the room.

'People like Brian May and Gary Barlow are guys I really respect, so it's amazing to be a part of it. I can't believe how nice all these guys have been to me – I really wasn't expecting any of it. I'm in slight shock,' he said afterwards.

Back at his new home, he was not only feeling better psychologically, he had started to get fit again after having a state-of-the-art gym installed.

'Since having the gym put in I've not stopped working

out. My brother Mike and I have been skipping, running and lifting weights,' he revealed.

'I've been pictured quite a lot recently and while people have been complimentary, I'm nowhere near how I want to look. After losing that weight I'm now determined to build myself up again and look ripped. Maybe not quite like I was in the "Mysterious Girl" video, though!'

As expected, with Peter's new suave image, there was plenty of speculation about his love life too. *Celebrity Big Brother* winner and Jordan lookalike Chantelle Houghton was the first woman Peter was linked to after they were spotted having dinner together after meeting at a designer's champagne launch party.

Peter fuelled the rumours further by writing in his *New!* magazine column the following week: 'Chantelle's a really lovely girl – a real sweetheart. We had such a great night and I think she's looking great at the moment.'

Although he clearly enjoyed being linked with the pretty blonde, he later denied they'd dated, saying he wasn't ready for a new woman in his life.

'The story about me and her dating was nonsense. She was a guest at a dinner I went to. I'm a highly sexed guy normally but I don't have the will at the moment.'

But in the midst of all the positive hype, there were some devastating moments for Peter. One of the first was Katie's revelation in her own interview with chat show host Piers Morgan that she'd had a miscarriage a few weeks before Peter had left her. The glamour model told in graphic detail how she lost her baby ten weeks into the pregnancy, but continued to run the London Marathon a week later because she didn't want to let down sponsors. Peter and Katie had believed she was pregnant while out in America but waited until they were back in the UK to have a scan.

'It was on the screen and the doctor said, "No, it's died, it's gone." He said, "Well, we can terminate it tonight. So I had to be there – I had to be put to sleep to have it terminated.

'It's dangerous to run when you're bleeding that much,' she continued, 'you can get a blood clot. On the day of the Marathon I keep going to the toilet because I keep checking to see if I'm bleeding. I'm trying to keep myself together, not cry. Four days after I lost the baby I ran the Marathon. And eight days later Pete told me he wanted a divorce. You'll have to ask Pete why,' she said.

In a follow-up interview, Katie – who was clearly still hurting from the ordeal – continued: 'If you haven't got your husband to help support you through such an awful situation that says a lot about the man. I've had nothing. Not one phone call expressing how sorry he is for the split or how I am feeling after the miscarriage or asking if I'm okay. As far as he knows I could have been sitting at home slitting my wrists.'

She added: 'It's not right for a man to leave a woman after they've just lost a baby after seeing a picture in a paper that triggers them to leave. There's one word for it – jealousy. Jealousy killed our relationship.'

Peter was incredibly upset, not just because of the potential backlash from fans after choosing to leave his wife following such a harrowing ordeal but because they had made a pact to keep it secret. They had lost other babies in the past, including one before Princess, and he couldn't understand why she had spoken out about this miscarriage over the other devastating incidents before.

He wrote in his magazine column: 'By revealing all about the baby we lost, Kate went against everything we said we'd never do.

'The miscarriage was a devastating time for us both, but I strongly believe it should have remained private. Unfortunately, what Kate says is out of my control.'

The singer was devastated by the way Katie had chosen so publicly to disclose their secret and in another sign of support, his parents flew halfway across the world from Australia to be with him on the day her shock revelation on Piers Morgan's show was broadcast on ITV.

As his estranged wife spoke out about the ordeal, Peter was out having dinner with his ever-supportive parents. Fortunately for the Andre family, there was no public outrage against Peter: it was simply viewed as another sad twist in the couple's unhappy marriage. It was also becoming clear by now that neither Peter nor Katie could reason; whatever one said, the other disputed and it had started as a one-on-one public and personal battle they were fighting.

But all that had changed when Katie met Alex Reid, a cage fighter, who just two short months after the split moved into the family home and into the marital bed. Now Katie had a wingman: Alex was a fighter, he craved the limelight and he seemed to have slotted in where Peter had left, just weeks before. Worst of all, the loved-up couple were being photographed playing happy families with his children and Pete wondered if he was going to be pushed out for good. Would there be any room for him in his kids' lives? Was this stranger about to win their hearts? It was his worst fears come true.

Not only that, it was dredging up some very dark emotions that Peter thought he'd manage to lay to rest a long time ago.

CHAPTER TEN
DIVORCE DILEMMAS

'It was my first panic attack in years, not when I heard they had got together but when I saw a photo of them all out as a family. It killed me. It was like you didn't just get stabbed in the heart, it got twisted and it got lifted. That was the moment I broke like I'd never broken. Seeing my children with another man? That moment was the worst moment.'

The panic attack seemed to come from nowhere and was terrifyingly powerful. Just hours before, Peter had opened a newspaper and to his horror saw snaps of his children on an idyllic day out in the countryside with his ex-wife and new man Alex. For all to see, the photos showed the muscle-bound hunk playing tennis and flying a kite with Harvey, Junior and Princess in a field near Katie's stables. At one point, the boxer threw Peter's giggling four-year-old Junior in the air before moving in for a kiss and cuddle with Kate. To the uninitiated, he looked like the children's father and to make matters worse, the kids seemed enamoured with their new playmate.

Peter had already been struggling with depressive thoughts after the split but this latest twist hit him hard.

'I woke up at two in the morning and I felt like I'd been hit on the head with a hammer and it was a horrible feeling,' he admitted months later.

'I went downstairs to tell my brother Mike that I might need to get to hospital, it was the same feeling that I had when I had meningitis. And just like that I passed out. I woke up later with blood all over my face – I must have hit something on the way down and was like, "What's going on?" and then I started to panic.'

As he lay on the floor in a daze it became clear to him that the fear of losing his children had put his body and mind under considerable stress.

'It was like being back in the day. I think seeing my kids with another man opened up a new emotion I didn't even know existed. I don't think it was him – it could have been anyone. He could have been a really nice guy, how would I know? I never met the guy.'

Up until this point and in tough circumstances, Peter had done everything to create as much of a secure, loving environment for his children. He had provided a warm and welcoming second home, told them that both he and Katie loved them very much and always kept his word with the promised weekend visits to ensure the reality of having estranged parents didn't hit them too hard. But suddenly there was a whole side to their lives that was completely out of his control.

And with the stories emerging about Alex and his seedy underworld past, it was no wonder Peter was anxious: the man playing Daddy hardly looked like a role model for his children.

Peter had already spoken out about his worries after seeing snaps of Alex and Katie groping and kissing each other in front of the kids in a Brighton park.

'God only knows what's going on in that house if they behave like that in a public park! I just hope my kids aren't being exposed to that behaviour every day,' he said at the time.

Kate had met Alex, a champion at the bloodthirsty sport of cage fighting, just 10 weeks after splitting from Peter after being introduced by her personal trainer, Sol Gilbert. After a wild night together in a Manchester hotel, secret liaisons at the family home followed and a fortnight later, Alex was already a permanent fixture in Katie's life.

Not shy of the limelight, the cage fighter (who had once starred as a footballer in Channel 4 soap *Hollyoaks*) joined Katie on her UK tour plugging her new book, *Sapphire*. But as Katie admitted to introducing him to their children over a roast chicken Sunday lunch, the torrid tales emerging of his past could only have sent shivers down Peter's spine. To be fair, Alex always appeared nothing but mild-mannered around his young family and the two men never publicly fell out – but on paper at least he was looking like the most undesirable person on the planet to have as a stepfather.

His ex-girlfriend of three years, Danielle Sims, said Alex was an insatiable sex maniac who liked to strangle her during wild S&M sessions. The boxer himself admitted to taking cocaine 'once too often' – which didn't go down well with staunchly anti-drugs Peter – and spoke of the gangsters he mixed with in the murky world of boxing as 'good people just bending some rules'.

Alex also cross-dressed as a woman called Roxanne to 'spice up' his sex life, something he confessed to Katie just two days after meeting her – but the mum-of-three fully embraced it.

'Call me strange, call me weird, call me whatever,' she told chat show host Graham Norton, a few months later. 'You name it, he's into it! He's only got one nipple because he used to put a clamp on it. Like he says, anything goes. I'm having such a fun time.'

But Peter didn't see the funny side, especially when it emerged his son Junior had seen his mum in bed with her new lover just a few weeks into the relationship. Katie denied point-blank that it had happened, but with the story splashed across the press it was another black mark against her name.

'Junior just said, "Why is he in bed with Mummy? What is he doing in Mummy's bed?" That's the most disgraceful thing I have ever heard. Ever,' Peter despaired in an interview at the time.

'I don't want to look like I am using the kids to have a dig at her but they should never ever be exposed to that kind of thing. To walk into that room, in that bed, with another man? That to me is the lowest blow ever. And for Junior to ask me about it? He's only four!' When it then emerged that his children's new father figure was starring in a vile and degrading hardcore porn movie, Peter was again justifiably appalled.

In *Killer Bitch*, Alex was filmed taking part in a shocking rape and strangulation scene.

'I can't believe he is making films like that. What kind of role model is he for my children?' said Peter.

He had heard enough and determined to keep a dignified silence wherever possible, he realised the only way to move on was to cut Katie out of his life. 'I have even taken off all my Google alerts and everything so I don't hear about her. She is a grown person and I can't control her. I have no feelings about what she's up to,' he told the *News Of The World*.

'Am I ready to find love again? I really don't think I want to be with someone in this industry. I might be wrong but once bitten, twice shy. Will I get back together with Katie? Never!'

Katie too was adamant that she was looking ahead to life without him.

'Splitting with Pete is the best thing that ever happened to me. There was a time when I was in pieces but that's all behind me now. All the time I was with Pete I was more concerned with making sure our marriage worked, but now I am focusing on me, my children and my career.'

But to make matters even more complicated, Katie was still calling Peter and sending late-night texts in apparent moments of despair.

'I don't want to say exactly what she said,' Peter revealed at the time. 'I just assume she'd had a bit too much to drink.'

Publicly, however, the war of words between him and Katie trundled on – everything from their marriage and their sex life to the children. When questioned about her new relationship with Alex, Katie couldn't help taking further swipes at Peter, including one in which she claimed sex was 'better than she was used to'.

Try as he might to ignore her, Katie was throwing a lot at him from saying she still had feelings for him, that Peter had dumped her to promote his music career to outlandish claims that his son Junior would cry when it was his turn to look after the children. Peter was confused too. 'I really don't know how to react to comments like this anymore,' he said of her story about Junior. 'Katie has been putting me down for five and a half years and it's a real shame she doesn't see fit to stop it now and we're not even together. She makes jibes at me constantly and it really upsets me.'

It also wasn't easy with Alex around, particularly when he heard that Harvey had started to call him 'Dad'. Harder still was the boxer's admission in *New!* magazine – in which Peter had his column – that he loved hanging out with the singer's children. He also claimed to be in love with Katie and 'have told her pretty much every day since we met'. Difficult as it was, with the divorce now looming, Peter tried to deal with it in the same manner as he had with other trying times that had peppered his life – by focusing firmly on his own family and career instead.

'I don't want to get into this tit-for-tat situation. Sometimes I'm not perfect and I do retaliate but only if something is said about my parenting skills or I've been accused of an affair. I'm moving on now and want to put this whole sorry affair behind me,' he declared. But the stress was clearly taking its toll in a telling speech at the Edinburgh International

Television Festival a few weeks before his divorce when Peter threatened to one day quit show business.

'There will come a point, I don't know how soon, that I won't want to do any of it anymore,' he told the audience. 'There might come a point where I don't want to be in this industry at all.'

Despite the obvious downsides to fame, Peter was still enjoying life as both a TV star and singer, and when the viewing figures for his and Katie's rival TV shows came through he was again coming out as a clear winner with the public. Excellently timed to be broadcast in the month running up to their divorce, Katie's show, *What Katie Did Next*, pulled in 1.5 million viewers while Peter's *Going It Alone* netted a victorious 1.7 million.

Katie took the news gracefully and this time at least there was no public spat over this particular battle. It may have been due, in part, to the fact there was now a complete communication breakdown between Peter and Katie, with conversations directed solely through their lawyers. The only time their paths seemed to cross was when handing over their children.

'We haven't been in touch for three weeks,' Peter admitted. 'All our communication now is done through lawyers. I'm not bothered who Kate dates, or who she's in a relationship with as long as it doesn't affect my children. Unlike Kate, I'm not going to have a divorce party, but good luck to her!'

However for a break-up so fraught with argument, when the day of Peter's divorce arrived, on 8 September 2009, there was not a squabble in sight. Under the guidance of top-notch lawyers Fiona Shackleton (who represented Paul McCartney in his divorce from Heather Mills) acting for Katie and Stephen Foster for Peter, the fuss-free proceedings were over in just 42 seconds. Under the names Price K v Andrea PJ – Peter's real surname – the couple had cross petitioned each other for a divorce on the grounds of unreasonable behaviour, meaning neither was held fully responsible.

At the High Court in London, District Judge Bradley granted a decree nisi in under a minute with neither Peter nor Katie present. Instead the singer was making his debut on ITV breakfast show *This Morning* as a showbiz reporter.

Host Eamonn Holmes asked him: 'Are you aware that you're getting divorced today?' to which a smiling Peter replied, 'Really? Well, yeah, just before I came in I was told that it's been accepted.'

That evening, he celebrated his new life as a bachelor, not with a rumoured divorce party, but by watching kids' movie *Toy Story* at home on the sofa with Junior and Princess.

It was another six weeks before the divorce was completely finalised but after their decree absolut was granted in mid-October, Peter was visibly relieved. On the driveway of his Brighton home, he was snapped hugging his older brother Michael and manager Claire, while clutching a set of legal papers. Choking back tears, he told them: 'It's over. It's been hard, but you guys have always been there for me. I'm stronger now, I can cope with anything.'

Much to his relief, along with the divorce came joint custody of the children, with Junior and Princess dividing their time between their parents. He was also allowed to look after disabled Harvey, then seven, for two days a fortnight.

With Peter owning the £2million villa in Cyprus and Katie their £3million family home in Woldingham, Surrey, the financial settlement – although never publicly confirmed – seemed relatively straightforward. Coupled with the fact Peter had insisted on a pre-nup, it was believed the only real negotiation was over divvying up shared property.

'It has been a hostile past few weeks but finally there is light at the end of the tunnel,' a friend revealed to the *Daily Mirror* a few days before. 'Peter and Katie are desperate not to delay proceedings. The divorce is not about money so there'll be no wrangles. Peter isn't really asking for any money or property from Katie, but there are a few pieces of furniture that he wants back.'

Relations with his former wife were now manageable, in so far as all negotiations and conversations could be controlled through a solicitor. Katie, however, clearly wanted to play something of a role in Peter's life and her provocative comments were still gaining his attention.

On the morning the divorce came through she gave an interview on *This Morning* implying the marriage had been nothing more than a business deal. 'Well, for me and Peter it is a business. We all know the entertainment business is a fake world, not a real world,' she said.

Not wishing for it to become another source of speculation, Peter rebutted her claims, saying: 'This has been the most heartbreaking year of my life. For her to think it was a business deal just sums her up.'

But Katie was clearly still struggling to cope and in a show of her true feelings for her ex, she made a last-ditch attempt to speak to Peter in person. It wouldn't have come as much of a surprise to the singer since he'd received several text messages in the days running up to the proceedings begging for a reconciliation.

'Katie texted me two weeks ago saying she is still in love with me,' he confessed to *OK!* magazine the day after their divorce.

Katie, meanwhile, sent out another clear message to Peter on the TV breakfast show, adding: 'All I want to do is meet up with Pete. All I'd like to say to Pete is "Let's just sit in a room, just us." I just don't hold anything against him. Let's just be adults. At the end of the day I just have to keep ringing solicitors to discuss the children. I just want to ring Pete.'

But Peter remained resolute. He wanted to be civil with Katie for the sake of their children but the clock couldn't be turned back.

Now, at long last, he was free to enjoy life as a single man and he confided to friends that one day soon he might be ready to find love again. Already there had been plenty of speculation over whether Peter had started dating again but bizarrely, most of the wild rumours linking him with a string of women had been put about publicly by Katie herself. All of them, he maintained, were false.

In two weeks alone, his ex accused him of sleeping with at least five different women, including the children's nanny, his longstanding manager Claire Powell and a variety of famous faces, including *X Factor* Essex girl Stacey Solomon.

As well as refuting the claims in his column branding them 'all lies', he joked in an interview a month after the divorce: 'I keep getting accused of having this secret girlfriend and I still look around the room and think, "Where is she?" I feel frustrated at all these silly playground put-downs linking me to different women.

'So far I'm supposed to have slept with my best mate Nik's wife Michelle Clack, Chantelle Houghton, Nicola McLean, Alesha Dixon, my manager Claire and my nanny! But for every person I've been accused of sleeping with, I'd take a lie-detector test and I'd be willing to stand up in court and swear on oath that it's not true. There will come a time where I'll be with someone and then I'll be told I was seeing them all along. You just can't win. But I don't have a girlfriend and I haven't slept with anyone.

'I'm not a prude but I don't want to rush into bed with just any girl,' he added. 'Yes, I'm a hot-blooded Greek guy and I'm like any other man but it hasn't been my priority since the split. I'm only 36 and I've just come out of a bitter divorce battle. I could meet someone today but I'm not planning it and I feel better about that because it gives me a sense of freedom. I enjoy being single.'

For the time being at least, life for Peter was about focusing on being a single Dad and he was clearly loving every minute he had with his children. Being a parent to Junior, four, and two-year-old Princess was giving him the strength to conquer his anxieties and look to the future.

'The children have definitely been my lifeline and my focus, and they got me through the divorce,' he said. 'It feels like I've been given a new lease of life. Now I've just got the kids, all of my attention is on them.

'I'm very firm with them but not as strict as my parents were with me. I believe in discipline and the naughty step works wonders!'

He was also enjoying the time he was allowed to spend with severely autistic Harvey and was relieved that the bond between them hadn't faded with all that had gone on. Although he cherished every moment they shared, it was hard not seeing him as often as he had done when married to Katie and the fact he wasn't the child's real father was starting to impact on him.

'Now I get to spend every other weekend and certain holidays with Harvey, but I have to respect the fact that he is not my child. As much as I would love to have him more, that is what I am being given permission for,' he said at the time.

However in a time of crisis, Peter was still a major figure in little Harvey's life, which was made all the more clear when the tot fell desperately ill and was rushed to hospital a month after the divorce.

Peter was heading to a Disney Store to switch on the Christmas lights when a frantic Katie called to say her eldest son had swine flu and the doctors were worried he would develop complications from the illness. The singer dropped everything and dashed to East Surrey Hospital to be by his bedside. It was the first time he and Katie had been together for any length of time since splitting and far from being a difficult meeting, they put on a united front for her son.

'All the horrible stuff in the last six months meant nothing at that moment,' Peter said afterwards. 'I went to the hospital and spent a few hours there but didn't stay the night. They let us stay longer than you're allowed. When it comes to your children, you don't think of anything else and I'm sure she didn't. It was amicable, we just spoke about the kids.'

Ironically, just four days after his poignant dash to Harvey's side, Peter's second single, 'Unconditional' from the album *Revelation*, was released in which he sings about his special relationship with Katie's son.

'The song "Unconditional" means the most to me. It was written about Harvey and the unconditional love I feel for him. Harvey taught me to be a father before I became a biological dad myself and I don't think anyone had written a song about that relationship before.'

Recorded in the same studio in America where Peter's hero Michael Jackson recorded with his gospel choir, the single, which includes a live choir and strings section, was the most expensive track to make on *Revelation*. Sadly, despite being tipped to top the charts, the album only reached No. 50 but it was still a hit with fans when Peter sung it for Children In Need, prompting millions of viewers watching the TV fundraiser to donate to the charity.

It was an emotional performance and again did wonders for his reputation, particularly since Katie was 12,000 miles away, battling it out in the Bushtucker Trials after returning to *I'm A Celebrity... Get Me Out Of Here!* for its ninth series.

Although something of a chart flop, Peter has always

maintained that it was worth every penny and every second he spent on the album, just so Harvey might one day discover he had a song written about him. It was important for the singer to somehow show Harvey what a massive impact he'd had on his life and in a manner that he would understand.

Over the years one of the ways Peter had nurtured their special bond was through music, discovering it was an easy way to communicate with the profoundly disabled boy. It hadn't been difficult for him to strike up a relationship with Harvey, it had been love at first sight on meeting him backstage at the *I'm A Celebrity...* launch before he and Katie went into the jungle for the first time.

'I knew Dwight his father would be involved and I knew the boy's grandmother Amy already played a very important role in his life but you can't help falling in love with him. Harvey responds well to music and now I'm not with him every day when I speak to him I will sing down the phone and he loves it. I hope that one day he will hear the song is for him and that means the world to me,' he said after the divorce.

Peter had witnessed first-hand the severity of Harvey's illness right from the start of his relationship with Katie and seeing him fall dangerously ill on many occasions each time served as a reminder of how important he was to him.

Speaking about one of those first frightening experiences, Peter said: 'One night within half an hour Harvey's temperature leaped from normal to near fatal. One minute he was playing with his toys, the next he was almost having an epileptic fit. This can happen to him and he can slip into a coma.

'His temperature was 39 degrees. Above 40 is fatal. I held Harvey, tears rolling down my face. "Please say something," I begged. "D-da-da," he mumbled. It broke my heart. All I could I think was, "My son, my son."'

With such an overwhelming love for Harvey, it made it all the more difficult when Katie banned her son from appearing in the video for the single.

The touching scene, in which the then seven-year-old tells Peter, 'I love you, Dad', was deleted from the promotional video because of an agreement with Katie, who rightly or wrongly decided she didn't want him to appear. At the time Peter's fans were outraged. But his agent Claire explained: 'Peter never wanted to use Harvey in the video – it's just a three-second clip of him telling Peter he loved him.

'It's out of our control. We have to respect Kate's decision.'

Meanwhile, Peter's ex was back on *I'm A Celebrity...* and it was becoming increasingly clear to viewers of the ITV1 show that she still had feelings for him after declaring she couldn't stay in the jungle because of the memories it was conjuring up. Not only that, after quitting the show after just seven days, she dumped her lover Alex live on TV.

She told hosts Ant and Dec on the show: 'I've done a lot of reflecting and I think it's best I'm on my own. I just don't want to be in a relationship.

She added: 'Every morning I'd look over and expect to see Pete and it was like all these good memories, then it would click and I'd think all these good memories are gone now, it's sad. I wanted to stay to the end, but emotionally it was really, really hard – probably because of the Pete part, the good memories.'

Astonishingly, Peter was one of the first people she called afterwards. 'She asked me if I'd been watching,' he admitted. 'I genuinely hadn't seen any of it. Then she told me she was ending her relationship with Alex. I said that was up to her.

'All I was interested in talking to her about was the children. She wanted to see them, but they were supposed to be with me. I told her it was absolutely fine, I understood how important it was. I was trying to be a fair parent.'

Despite offering an olive branch to Katie in handing over the children when she returned to Britain, the period of goodwill didn't last long when she refused to let Peter take the family to Australia for Christmas.

Pete had wanted to take Junior and Princess to see his now seriously ill father Savva in Sydney, in what he feared would be a last reunion with his grandchildren. But when Katie vetoed the idea and the pair couldn't come to a compromise they ended up in court.

After a fierce custody battle at London's Family Court in Holborn, central London, which cost over £100,000 in legal costs and fees, the judge ruled in Katie's favour. Peter was seen leaving the court through a back door, looking 'rock bottom' and bleary-eyed.

'This has ruined Christmas, which is all about family. Nothing else matters,' he confided to pals. 'My dad was so looking forward to seeing the kids. He's not in the best of health so this could be the last time they might get to cuddle him. I've never felt so low. I fear this nightmare will go on forever.'

The pair finally came to an agreement where Peter had the children until teatime on Christmas Day before he flew out alone to Australia the following morning.

'I was devastated and tried to fight legally, but in the end I had to accept it and instead I got to see them in the run-up to Christmas and Christmas Day, which was amazing, before flying out the next day. It's that situation with the kids that had been killing me over the past months,' he admitted afterwards.

And it was becoming increasingly obvious that the nightmare over their parental differences was set to continue when on New Year's Eve the children were caught up in a drunken brawl at the family home.

While Peter was 11,000 miles away in Sydney, Katie threw a lavish £20,000 party, which erupted in violence when her back-on lover Alex came to blows with her ex, Dane Bowers.

Record producer Dane had reportedly picked a fight with Katie for allowing Junior and Princess to stay up past midnight before calling Alex a 'big ponce'. The row ended up in a punch-up before Katie threw them both out of the house.

Peter was understandably concerned. 'He is furious,' a friend confided. 'He can't believe anybody would go off like that with kids in the house. Little children should not be exposed to this and they shouldn't have even been there – they should be enjoying themselves in Australia with their dad.'

But the incident had happened and Peter was clearly learning to forgive, forget and move on.

Tanned, radiating confidence and fitter than ever, he returned from Australia having regained some of the three stone he lost during the break-up. He was ready to take on the world again and after 20 years in the business he had a new 38-date tour to look forward to, as well as another album in the pipeline.

2010 was to herald a new start for the star as he embarked on life as a bachelor again. Although now a responsible father, when it came to women the singer was also about to sample something of the wild days of his youth. But for now, Peter was justifiably proud. Throughout the divorce, the custody battles and the constant mudslinging with his ex, he had achieved the unthinkable: transforming himself from cheesy pin-up to credible artist, with more fans than ever before.

'I'm happy in a way I haven't been since my 20s. I felt my identity returning to me. I spent two weeks in Australia at Christmas with my family and friends. I did nothing but relax, chat, go out for dinner, play backgammon with my dad and sit in the sun,' he told *Fabulous* magazine.

'I was away from everything, all the madness. I felt my identity returning to me. I accepted the end of my relationship a long time ago, but I found it hard to come to terms with the place that left me in.

'Now I'm finally happy in myself. I think I've found the real me.'

CHAPTER ELEVEN

THE BOY IS
BACK IN TOWN

Peter was a man on a mission. No sooner had he returned to the UK then he was gearing up for what was to be the busiest year of his career.

He didn't know it yet, but he was set to perform to 100,000 fans on his *Revelation* tour and would notch up more major concerts in the UK than any other artist that year, overtaking Status Quo, JLS and even Westlife.

For the time being, he was focusing on the release of his new album, *Unconditional Love Songs*, a combination of his own material and covers. He was also rehearsing like mad with Michael Jackson's choreographer Sean Cheesman for the epic 38-date sell-out tour in the spring. With hundreds of letters from fans pouring through his letterbox every day, the singer was driven to succeed more than ever before.

To ensure he had input in every aspect of the production, Peter was designing the shows to be as impressive as the circus-inspired *Insania* tour but with a 'more grown-up, adult feel' to them. The performance was to include a special Michael Jackson tribute piece to his all-time hero, who had died the previous summer. Wanting it as personal as possible, Pete's brothers would be joining him onstage for a jam.

It seemed like all that had been important to the singer in his *annus horribilis* of 2009 was being pulled together in one giant room for one big party – his family, his fans and a tribute to the man who had inspired his entire career.

'A year and a half ago I was voted Celebrity Tool Of The Year. Looking back, I was a different person, I felt like a lot of the time I was a total mug,' he explained in the tour's run-up.

'What's been incredible is all the public support – that's helped more than I can say. At the end of each show on my tour, I'm going to thank the public for the life they've given me back. So much of how I feel now has to do with their support. I get letters, even food sent to me. It's unbelievably touching.'

Peter's children, Junior and Princess, were also getting involved in the pre-show hype and his son was hanging out at rehearsals practising the Michael Jackson routine alongside him. The bond between them was now closer than ever and Junior clearly enjoyed the limelight even more than his famous dad.

'JJ is such a little showman. He came up onstage with me in rehearsals and actually he upstaged me! The crew went wild – I think he has more fans than me! I joked that instead of it being *Peter Andre: Revelation* it should be *Junior Andre: Revolution* and sure enough, it was. Junior loved it – I think he'd like to be on stage himself one day although we'll discuss that nearer the time!' he said.

Peter was also keen to include his mum and dad in his successes back in the UK and as he approved items of merchandise for the tour, he had samples of brochures, mugs and T-shirts flown back home to Australia.

As if the dad-of-two wasn't busy enough, tending to his career and family, Peter was finally showing his wilder side. With the divorce out of the way, he finally waved goodbye to months of celibacy by embarking on a secret, passionate fling with a blonde model.

Maddy Ford, a former Page 3 girl-turned-stylist, met Peter at a children's birthday party hosted by mutual friends, champion windsurfer Nik Baker and his wife Michelle Clack, for one of their sons. A few weeks later the pair were invited back to the sportsman's home in Littlehampton, Sussex for a dinner party and Peter ended up staying over for a raunchy night in the couple's spare room.

It was a far cry from the way he had conducted his flings in his 20s when he picked up women in swanky nightclubs and at after-show parties. Nevertheless, Maddy was smitten and by all accounts Pete still had stamina between the sheets.

'I felt really nervous about sleeping with him because Katie Price comes across as such a sexual person. I thought she was probably an animal in bed,' she revealed to a newspaper. 'But Pete told me, "It's all an act. She's not like that at all." He told me I had the best body he had ever seen and that my breasts and bum were perfect. He made me feel good.

'Pete blew me away in bed. I know Jordan once claimed his manhood was the size of an acorn but that is categorically not true. Peter was perfect in every way.'

In a bid to keep their fling under wraps the pair managed to start working together and soon after returning from his New Year's break in Australia, stunning Maddy was hired to dress Pete for a commercial for his *Unconditional Love Songs* album. None of the crew realised their secret, even when he asked her later that day to appear as his lover in the video for a single taken off the record, 'I Can't Make You Love Me'.

'Peter had just come back from Australia and it was hard to keep our hands off each other. We were shooting a commercial for his album. I dressed him in a see-through jumper, a vest and jeans. I thought he looked sexy and stylish.

'At the end of the day we filmed a video for "I Can't Make You Love Me" and he gave me a part in it to act as his love interest but he insisted that my hair was tied in a bun because he said otherwise I looked too much like Katie, who'd been with him before in a similar pop video,' she revealed.

Publicly, however, Peter was still insisting he was single, saying he was holding out for 'The One'.

'I'm hoping it will hit me like a ton of bricks,' he said at the time, 'I'm a 36-year-old man with children and I want someone who is prepared to take all of that on. But it's all about the right girl. I want true love, a love that will last.'

Despite their clandestine sex sessions, it was obvious Maddy hoped they had a future together despite acknowledging Peter was still preoccupied with his ex and the life he had left behind.

'Pete was still very raw when it came to Katie. That's the best way to describe it. He talked about her a lot and there was a lot of point scoring.

'He told me that when she left *I'm A Celebrity...*, she phoned him and asked him if he would give their marriage another go. But he told her: "No, never." Then he'd say to me: "Maddy, you are so naturally beautiful, you don't need to wear make-up like she does." He would compare me to her like that. But I have fake boobs and wear false eyelashes, just like Katie!'

And Peter obviously didn't want to rush things. The tattoo on his wedding finger that spelt out the name 'Katie' remained.

'I don't want to have it removed because it would confuse my children,' he explained at the time. 'They look for it on my hand. When I meet the right woman it will go and I'll explain why, but for now it's there and I'm okay with that.'

His relationship with Maddy was clearly nothing more than a fling to him and he was desperate to keep it quiet. As well as protecting his children, he wanted to avoid the sort of sordid headlines his ex-wife had become renowned for since their split. Sadly it didn't work out that way and their love affair was splashed across the press when smitten Maddy spilled the beans after Peter told her it was over. The singer was furious with the unwanted attention and confessed at the time: 'Yes, it's true. I was intimate with Maddy on a handful of occasions. We both went into it with our eyes open, and let's just say I certainly know how to pick 'em!'

He added in another interview: 'I dipped my toe in the water and got burnt. I'm gutted. But I've got it out of my system. I don't want to go there with anyone else again now, not unless I know it's serious. The children are my priority.'

It was no surprise he wanted to devote his time to Junior and Princess. After all, the revelations about his secret sex life had come just a few weeks following what had been an extremely stressful time for Peter.

The day after the release of his much-anticipated album, *Unconditional Love Songs*, his ex-wife Katie had married Alex in a secret Las Vegas wedding.

Peter had already been furious after the loved-up pair had seemingly jetted off to America for a last-minute lucrative photo shoot after the cage fighter won Channel 4's reality TV show *Big Brother* – leaving the children behind. After finding out from the nanny that his ex had snuck off to Heathrow for a romantic break instead of looking after Harvey, Junior and Princess as planned, a friend said: 'Pete dropped the kids off at school as agreed on Monday morning. He has had them since Wednesday so Kate could have her weekend with Alex.

'Kate was meant to pick them up after school yesterday but word filtered back that she was on her way to Heathrow for a flight and the nannies would be looking after the kids all week. Pete hit the roof.'

But all became clear when at 10.30pm the following

evening he received a phone call, saying Katie's hushed-up dash to Las Vegas had been to marry in secret. She and Alex had tied the knot in one of the city's famous chapels in a quickie ceremony before checking into the £6,000-a-night honeymoon suite at the five-star Planet Hollywood hotel. No one else had been invited and Katie had kept it a secret from everyone, including her family.

At midnight, Katie's agent released in a statement: 'Kate and Alex are delighted to announce that they got married in a private, simple ceremony at 4pm (local time) on February 2nd in Las Vegas. Their reason for getting married is purely down to their love for each other.'

It came as a shock to everyone and none more so than Peter, who just 12 hours after hearing the news broke down while being interviewed live on TV. He had been booked to chat on *Sky News* about his upcoming new tour and album but when the interview immediately turned to his ex-wife, the singer lost his temper before walking off set.

Asked if he knew about the marriage, he replied: 'I didn't know. About 10.30 I got a phone call saying, "It's believed..."

'But it's not my business, I guess. To be honest, I wasn't surprised at all and, just like any other parent, I just want a good influence on my children.'

As the interview became increasingly emotionally charged, Peter was asked if his children had been told of their mum's wedding. Clearly feeling the strain, he said: 'Not from me. I haven't got to that point yet – that's something I've got to explain.'

But it became too much for him when interviewer Kay

Burley suggested Katie's new husband might adopt Junior and Princess. Breaking down in tears, Peter said: 'Nobody is going to take my kids away from me and I will fight to the death for that! Nobody's going to take those kids away – I'll die before I let that happen! It's not going to happen. I will go to court.'

But the normally laid-back singer really blew his top after he was shown an archive clip of Harvey's father, soccer legend Dwight Yorke, branding Peter 'disrespectful' for wanting to adopt his son.

Pete – who had been told he was about to see the video – hit back: 'No disrespect, but has he seen Harvey since that interview? I love that child, I see that child, and to me a nice little "thank you" would be nice. I asked to adopt him because I loved him, I didn't ask to adopt him to be disrespectful.

'When you love a child, he's in my life, he calls me "Dad". I never said I'm his father, but I'm so proud to have him in my life. Why is it disrespectful that I asked to look after someone's child? I'm sorry, but that angers me.'

Distraught, Pete then stopped the interview, saying: 'I don't really want to talk about this, okay? I'd rather just stop this, if that's all right.'

When the presenter tried to ask him about his tour, Pete was too upset and left the studio live on air.

'I'm very much Team Andre,' Burley wrote on her blog later as complaints rolled in, accusing her of bullying the much-loved star, 'Peter broke down on my show and when I went to check during an ad break that he was okay, he sobbed on my shoulder in the Green Room.'

Peter couldn't stop the tears, not because Katie had got married but because he was terrified about the negative effect this would all have on his children.

'It's all a bit of a blur to me now but at the time I was extremely upset, the interviewer really hit a raw nerve,' he said, years later. 'She could have asked me anything, but she brought the children into it. Perhaps some people thought I was upset about Katie getting married but that wasn't the case. I was genuinely pleased she had found someone and that she is happy but I'm still weak when it comes to the kids.'

Once again, the public rallied round, with 881 complaints made to the broadcasting regulator OFCOM and many writing in to newspapers and calling TV shows to express their horror at the way he had been treated.

Even Katie spoke out in his defence on her return to the UK, saying: 'Pete's an amazing dad to Harvey. He's his dad, and always will be. It upset me that they compared the two because Dwight has never played the role of dad in Harvey's life.'

Peter also gained some reassurance from Alex himself, who also praised the singer when appearing on Alan Carr's *Chatty Man* show, saying: 'How could I adopt them? Peter's a great dad – I don't want to take anything away from him, so why not all sit round a table? I am now officially a stepdad, it's surreal. I love those little kids, but I don't want to be their dad like Peter Andre.'

Much to Peter's relief, it was quite clear everyone was being careful not to make life any more difficult for the children than it was already and both he and Alex were not saying too much about each other to keep the peace too. He did, however, allow himself a few swipes about his ex-wife's marriage in his new reality ITV2 show, *The Next Chapter*. In a conversation with his brother Mike about the nuptials, he said: 'It's a complete joke, but good luck if that's what makes her happy. But it's quite hilarious!'

Not only was he finding humour in the latest dramatic turn of events, Peter was also taking further steps to move on after his wife's second marriage by having the tattoo on his wedding finger lasered off at a Brighton clinic. It was as much a physical gesture as a symbolic one; he was once more becoming his own man. Even better, his career was truly flourishing too.

In the seven days running up to the launch of his sell-out tour, Peter's manic timetable included five album signings, appearing on breakfast show *GMTV*, co-hosting ITV1's *This Morning* and sitting through scores of magazine and newspaper interviews. He also co-presented the prestigious BRIT Awards for ITV2 with radio DJ Fearne Cotton, again a measure of how far he had come in becoming a credible artist in the eyes of the music industry.

The album had peaked at No. 7 in the UK charts and went silver after selling over 65,000 copies, and the usually harsh critics were responding well to it too.

'The tragedy is that the man who tainted the world with "Mysterious Girl", and wrote the misunderstood jungle classic, "Insania", isn't without talent. Yes, talent,' wrote one BBC critic. 'Many of the songs here jut their bottom lip towards The Stylistics' soul flourishes and Michael Jackson's smooth balladry – indeed, "She's Out of My

Life" is covered here almost spiritually – and Andre's voice is sometimes charming; certainly an improvement on many of his ripped-ab pop contemporaries.'

The launch of his much-anticipated tour was no disappointment either. Headlines screamed 'pandemonium' as hordes of fans turned out to see the chart-topping pin-up, 'Team Andre' T-shirts were flying off the merchandise stalls and the auditorium went wild with screams of 'We love you!' as he thanked them for saving his life through the divorce.

On the opening night in Clacton, Essex, 3,000 fans stampeded the stage, with two needing medical treatment, as they clamoured to get closer to the singer as he paid his promised emotional tribute to the audience.

'As Peter said "thank you" the crowd really seemed to react to his message. They knew what he meant. He has been through so much this year and could not have got through it all, if it were not for his fans,' a journalist wrote in one concert review.

Footage of his father Savva and children projected above the stage as he sung 'Unconditional' went down a storm, as did his Michael Jackson medley, which had become something of a highlight for Peter in the show's running order.

'I was honoured that Sean Cheesman, Michael's choreographer, agreed to work with me. He'd done several of his videos, like *Scream*, *The Way You Make Me Feel* and *Bad*. Without him it wouldn't have been half the show it turned out to be. I wanted it to be as spot-on as possible, to make the King of Pop proud.

'The tour was a huge success and the hard work, long hours and effort paid off. It was a proper production and I had input into every aspect of it; it was so exhilarating to be part of that and to know it was my vision,' he said afterwards.

News was also coming through that his arena tour was quickly selling out, including a massive 18,000-capacity gig at London's O2, which was being billed as the 'gig of his life'. His album signings were also drawing in massive crowds to high street stores, with security teams and police needed to ensure the thousands of fans were kept under control.

Realising how important it was to give something back to his supporters, Peter would often stay for hours after his scheduled appearance to make sure he got to meet everyone who had turned up. At one signing a staggering 10,000 fans had queued round the block for hours to see him so Peter stayed until midnight to make sure no one went home disappointed.

'I have to pinch myself when I think that they are there to see little old me. They always cheer me up and make me smile. However many hours I have scheduled for the signings I always manage to over-run, not just by a few minutes but in many cases hours. I know I cause my management headaches,' he joked at the time.

It was like the Peter Mania of yesteryear, except when his work was over for the day, the wild parties and sleeping with scores of women had been swapped for domestic bliss and an 'early night' back at his Brighton home.

Days off work spelled time with the children – getting

them up, giving them their breakfast, going out for the day, making them tea – and Peter wanted to make sure he didn't miss a thing.

Although he enjoyed the rare night out, most of his social life revolved around movie nights in with friends, as well as cooking meals for the children and his brother Mike, who was living with him, as well as hosting barbecues in the summer.

'I love to do things that everyone else loves to do. Don't get me wrong, I do love to throw parties at the house occasionally but never if the kids are there. If I'm not working, I love to get an early night. The glamour stops when I get back from work, whether that's rehearsals or a launch or a signing, and I'm often tucked up in my 8ft bed by 10pm.

'When the kids are at home they'll ask if they can stay in with me and we'll climb in and watch a film together – it's bliss. It isn't that exciting, chez Andre!' he admitted.

And it was testament to his down-to-earth parenting that he was crowned Dad of the Year soon after the end of his tour – even beating Prime Minister David Cameron in the public vote. Coming a year after his split from Katie, winning the competition run by the charity Bounty was the icing on his cake.

'This means a huge amount to me as being a dad is my most important role. This feels so good. It's been a turnaround year for me and the kids, and it's an honour to be the subject of the public's support and best wishes,' he said.

The prize was made all the more sweeter when a few

days later on Father's Day he was reunited with Harvey after a two-month ban by Katie. She had stopped Peter from seeing him until he hired a qualified nanny to help look after Harvey when staying at his home, meaning the singer had missed out on the tot's 8th birthday celebrations. Peter had missed him terribly and when the former couple's very public war of words over Harvey came to an end, Peter told *OK!* magazine: 'It took two and a half months to find the right nanny, which felt like forever. Seeing Harvey again was amazing. I threw a joint birthday party for him, Junior and Princess, with rock-climbing, a trampoline, slides, soft play and all their friends.

'I've missed Harvey terribly – we have a great bond. I love him to bits and I always will.'

Although Peter and Katie's lives were now very separate the children continued to be a flashpoint. He was outraged when toddler Princess appeared on Katie's reality ITV show wearing false eyelashes and make-up. When the snaps were later posted on Facebook by Kate's sister Sophie and her best friend Gary Cockerill, Peter admitted it was more difficult to see than watching his ex-wife get remarried.

'If I'm to be honest, I'm absolutely disgusted. It's a two-year-old girl with false eyelashes, full make-up for the whole world to see, dressed like that. I don't want to see it,' he said.

Although the pair were at least communicating now in person, there was certainly no trust between them and Peter refused to call Katie about the incident fearing she would leak every detail. He explained to ITV breakfast show *GMTV*: 'If I pick up a phone, what will be said will not remain private. Usually when I come on I just talk about other things and I'm like, "Yeah, I'm not bothered and all this." But that did bother me.'

He continued to act as the rock for his young family, however, which was becoming increasingly important while their mother's personal life was undergoing such rapid changes. Five months after her shock nuptials in Las Vegas, the glamour model and cage fighter hosted another wedding – this time for friends and family, with a church blessing. But in true Katie style, the day descended into chaos after her arrival at the church in an A-team van and a £2,000 puffball wedding dress sparked a violent brawl.

Police were called in as a scuffle between security and photographers kick-started a massive fight in which well-wishers and guests were caught up in the scrum. After the 15-minute ceremony, Alex's cage-fighting pals were also said to wade into the erupting violence outside, with one snapper claiming one threw a cigarette in his face.

Thankfully for Peter, he was thousands of miles away in Marbella, Spain at the time, shooting a new calendar. It was just as well for in what was seen as a final snub to the singer, the wedding reception was held in the garden of the former marital home. Even if that had been Katie's intention, it was to have little effect on Peter. The singer had already been careful to distance himself from the event and had even gone so far as to give it his blessing by telling Junior to 'give Mummy a kiss from me' before going to the ceremony. Peter had told friends he was pleased that his five-year-old son and Princess, three, were so excited about the big day and thought it only appropriate to show his support.

With his packed work schedule, distancing himself from Katie's seemingly exhausting antics was probably as much out of necessity as it was emotionally since Peter had plenty on his plate. Life was treating him well career-wise and financially; he had been offered – but turned down because of his UK commitments – a judging role on Australia's version of *The X Factor* and had splashed out on a new £2million home in West Sussex.

The sprawling mansion was just what the singer had been looking for and was set in a picturesque spot where famous neighbours included Hollywood star Tom Cruise.

'He's been on the hunt for a new place for months and he's taken the plunge. It's a brand new house with seven bedrooms so there's plenty of space for the kids and the rest of the family. It has every luxury inside, it's peaceful and gives lots of privacy – just the place to start afresh,' a friend revealed.

And that was exactly what Peter appeared to be doing.

Since the divorce, the singer had vowed to look after himself a bit more by putting into place a series of measures to stay healthy, including eating well, resting often and keeping fit. He had no desire to return to the extreme dieting and 500 press-up routines of the nineties, which preceded his massive emotional breakdown. But despite being kind to himself, both physically and mentally, his life was still peppered with anxiety attacks, suffering up to 20 times a day and forcing him to hide away in bed. At least he knew how to live with them now and they no longer paralysed him with fear.

In an interview with Irish radio station Newstalk 106, he said: 'You learn to deal with them. They're very cheeky little things, they're your enemy and your friend. They'll tap you on the shoulder once in a while to let you know they're still there. They remind me not to take life for granted or get too cocky.'

He was clearly becoming a dab hand at dealing with stress but nothing could prepare him for an incident just a few days after Katie's second wedding to Alex. The singer was out on a jog at 5.30am near his home when he collapsed in agony, fearing he was having a heart attack. He had been struck with a bolt of pain to his chest, forcing him to slump to the ground. A passer-by helped him back to his house and his brother Mike called an ambulance.

'I'd only been running for about 10 minutes when I suddenly had the most excruciating, stabbing pains in my chest.

'I couldn't breathe properly and immediately thought I was having a heart attack. It was that bad, I thought I was dying,' he explained to *New!* magazine.

However, when paramedics turned up they found he had a torn ligament in his chest, which had caused similar symptoms to cardiac failure. Peter decided against going to hospital for monitoring, but was left terrified by the incident.

'It was a really nasty experience. By that point though, I was keen to rest at home so I stayed put,' he explained.

The singer also had a busy schedule to press ahead with and although his health and mental wellbeing was these days at the top of his agenda, the show also had to go on. Peter was now being hailed the 'darling of ITV' after being signed up for a third series of his ITV2 show, *The Next Chapter*, after regularly pulling in more than 1.2million viewers. He was also launching a new perfume for women called 'Mysterious Girl' after his chart-topping hit, while working hard on his new single 'Defender', which again heralded another musical direction for him.

The track was initially released online as a digital download, with a physical release the following day exclusive to supermarket ASDA, which had boldly snapped up 100,000 copies.

'Releasing this was a big risk for me because it's so different,' 37-year-old Peter admitted on the day of its release, 'But I'm all about pushing boundaries. I'd never have thought I'd be releasing an album at this age!'

The track, which he had premiered on the live final of BBC's *Strictly Come Dancing* following in the footsteps of Robbie Williams and Gary Barlow, who had also sung on the show, peaked at No. 14 in the singles charts. It was quickly followed by his album, *Accelerate*, which was released a month before his December arena tour.

The 'urban pop' record produced and mixed by Pete 'Boxsta' Martin, best known for his work with the Sugababes, and executively produced by Warren Askew, who discovered Estelle, heralded a new edgier R&B style, which Peter hoped would help crack the American market. It also saw him collaborate with R&B sensations

Labrinth and Taio Cruz and world-renowned songwriter, Guy Chambers.

'This album is so different. I've got my TV show and my scent, so I figured I can afford to take a risk with my music,' he said at the time. 'It was a tough decision to go with the UK urban sound. I was like, "Is this going to be a flop?" Everyone knows that Michael Jackson is my biggest inspiration but I wanted to nod to what's on in the charts today.'

But he needn't have worried for his 'happy, feel-good album' was well received, reaching a respectable No. 10 in the UK album charts, with over 125,000 copies sold.

Hot on its heels, his first arena tour in 15 years had sold out, extra dates had been added and his own team had moaned they couldn't book a corporate box at the O2 because of overwhelming demand.

'For the show, we've got the producer and director from *Thriller* in the West End, the choreographer from *StreetDance*, and visually it's great because we've got guys who have worked with George Michael and Prince, so we're putting on a first-class show. I'm so thrilled with it.' Peter said.

But after months of gruelling rehearsal and literally thousands of hours of painstakingly precise preparations, the opening night was struck by disaster. Just a few hours before the launch of the tour at the Plymouth Pavilions, Peter was rushed to hospital in excruciating pain.

In a statement posted on his official website, his manager wrote: 'We are very worried about Peter and at present we do not know what is causing him to be in so much pain. Peter is terribly disappointed that he is unable to perform at tonight's sold-out opening night. At this time we have no more information.'

Peter had been found by his road manager on all fours and riddled with pain in his hotel room just before going to rehearse for the evening's show. He had also started to pass blood and after being rushed to Taunton's Musgrove Park Hospital in Somerset, doctors battled to discover the reason behind the singer's mystery stomach ailment. Finally he was diagnosed with suffering from kidney stones.

In the meantime, Peter was terrified as he was reminded of the hell he had gone through after being struck down with meningitis.

After an emergency operation, doctors told him to rest but determined not to let down the fans, 48 hours later he performed at Butlins in Minehead, Somerset. Under doctor's orders not to dance, Peter belted out some of his hits sitting down and afterwards dashed home to rest. Mentally drained, he tearfully admitted to friends he wanted to see his children, who were staying with Katie at the time.

The episode had also taken its toll on the singer physically and to his horror the performance left him with internal bleeding and he was forced to postpone a second date. However, after another consultation with medics he was given the green light to continue his tour and Team Andre was up and running again at full pelt.

Little did the sell-out crowds realise that behind Peter's smile and high octane dance routines, he was still recuperating from the kidney operation and his concerts had to be specially adapted so he could run offstage whenever he needed to alleviate his symptoms, though.

'It was great to be back, but I had to use a trap door on the stage so I could run off for a wee in an emergency,' he revealed months later.

It hadn't been easy for him, but his hard work paid off and the two-hour shows were hailed a storming success, with a set list containing a mix of old and new songs, with chart-topper 'Mysterious Girl' as an encore. But for the singer, the greatest highlight was his gig-of-a-lifetime at London's O2. As a child, Peter had always dreamed of performing at Wembley in front of a 12,500-capacity crowd, but this newer arena was now the largest in London and 20,000 fans crammed in to see him.

'My dream came true recently when I did my first gig at The O2 arena in London,' he said. 'It's a massive venue and the gig was completely sold out, so there was quite a crowd, to say the least. I can't tell you how amazing it felt to perform there. It was just unbelievable. I was over the moon.'

The shows also proved how far he had come in more ways than just musically. His punishing pre-show routines of the nineties, where he practically starved himself before performing 500 sit-ups, were long gone. Now he had just one vice, something he relied on to kick-start every set – a shot of espresso just before stepping on stage.

Once there, he now had his brother Mike and Chris join him for some of his performances beneath impressive pyrotechnics while footage of Peter and his children was projected onto the backdrop.

And the singer cranked up the family-vibe still further at his Cardiff Arena show by introducing his son to the screaming crowds as they performed Michael Jackson's 'Moonwalk' together.

It was a symbolic moment. Not only had he achieved his teenage dream of performing in some of the world's largest arenas, but he was now a proud father himself – and a good one at that. It was proof indeed that Peter had finally made his mark as a credible artist, but ironically now he was achieving that, what had become far more important to him was how he was perceived as a father.

'I can handle someone saying they hate my music or don't like my style. When people come up and tell me I'm a good dad that means so much.

'After all this time, I've realised the ultimate compliment is someone thinking you're a good bloke,' he said after one of the shows.

But the public wasn't just interested in his music and role as Dad, Peter was a pin-up and interest in his love life had reached fever pitch.

He had declared celibacy following his fling with Maddy Ford at the start of the year and even joked after a show in Edinburgh when a fan gave him a giant teddy that 'This is the only creature allowed in my bed from now on!' But half a year later, Peter had caved in to desire and was back on the dating scene; he was finally ready for a serious relationship.

'There's a saying that you have to kiss a few frogs before you find your prince. In my way, maybe I have to kiss a few tadpoles before I meet my princess,' he tried to explain. 'The people I've dated are wonderful and I really want to bring that across because that's really important. What I should say is you can't just jump into something – you have to get it right.'

So who would be the one to last the distance and take on pop's number one family man? It remained a mystery but in a strange twist of fate, one of the most horrendous moments of the past year was set to lead him onto a path to the woman he wanted to spend the rest of his life with.

On the night he had fallen desperately ill with kidney stones, a urology consultant at Musgrove Park Hospital, Dr Ruaraidh 'Ru' MacDonagh, had performed emergency surgery on the star and the pair immediately struck up a firm friendship. Over the next few years, Peter would join the world-class surgeon at charity events and the singer, along with his children, would regularly visit Ruariadh's family – which included his beautiful daughter, Emily.

Peter was to eventually fall for the medical student and the fairytale ending of which the singer was daring to dream would finally be in his grasp. But all that was not to be for another two years. For now, he was still having fun trying to find his princess and there seemed to be quite a few potential Mrs Andres in the frame...

CHAPTER TWELVE
LOOKING FOR LOVE

Peter was relieved, his once-burning love for Katie had completely diminished and finally, he felt ready to plunge headfirst into a relationship.

'For the first few months after [the divorce] I was confused and must have had some sort of love but when it went, it was instant. I woke and thought, "Oh wow, it's a bright day!" It was gone. I'm absolutely 100 million per cent certain that there's no love there whatsoever.'

After the kiss-and-tell fiasco with Maddy Ford, he decided the best way to maintain some control over having his secrets splashed across the press was to come clean himself when he started seeing women again.

One of his first conquests was his ex-wife's former assistant Angela Mogridge, a stunning Australian he had known for over 10 years – and a woman he would most probably be with today, if it wasn't for the fact they lived on opposite sides of the world. Peter had been drawn to her from day one but after a decade of never having the opportunity to act on his instincts, once his divorce was out of the way the pair finally embarked on a sizzling fling.

He had first met the ex-girlband star through his brother Michael and they were reunited on the set of *I'm A Celebrity...* in 2004 when she assisted Katie in her role as celebrity chaperone on the ITV1 show. The chemistry between them was unmistakeable and they swapped numbers with a view to meeting up once the TV programme had finished. But when Peter started dating Katie straight after being booted out of the jungle, the singer cut off all contact with the pretty blonde.

'I got rid of every number, including Angela's. A couple of months after the split, I started getting back in touch. Prior to my marriage nothing ever happened with Angela. Now I can say she's a great girl – we have a mutual love and respect,' he said after confirming they were dating.

Peter finally bedded Angela, now a graphic designer, after she came to visit his brother Michael in London and on meeting her again the singer realised that she was actually the 'perfect woman' he'd been looking for. But there was one crucial snag: she lived in Australia and Peter had a life back in the UK with his children.

'Ange is the girl who absolutely ticks every box,' he said at the time. 'Except the box that says: "Doesn't live hundreds of thousands of miles away". I've told her that. We talk about it, but it's hard to ask someone to move their whole life to see if something will work out. Who knows what's going to happen? You just have to believe in fate.

Angela is one of the nicest girls I've ever met. We've always been attracted to one another.'

Despite coming clean about the romance, Peter suffered a backlash when he was accused in October 2010 of leaking details of the relationship as a 'publicity stunt' on the same day his new single, 'Defender', was out. He was also slated by Katie's online fanbase for being insensitive in dating one of her 'friends'.

But Peter was quick to dismiss the accusations and told pals: 'Angela is nothing to do with my ex, they hardly know each other. She frisked Katie before she went into the jungle to check she wasn't hiding anything in her clothes but that's as far as it went.

'Who cares if I have had sex? I am a single guy and have been more than admirable, I would never shamelessly talk about my sex life for publicity.'

But the relationship with Angela was never to be anyway; despite their mutual desire, the two went their separate ways. The distance between them meant one of them needed to take the massive risk of leaving the life they'd built for themselves for a long-term relationship that might not go the distance. 'We did say we'd be together if she lived in England or I lived in Oz. Now she's getting on with her life and I'm getting on with mine,' he said after their split.

With another girl out of the picture, there was no end of speculation about who Peter was sharing his intimate time with. Ex-Sugababe Keisha Buchanan was one of his friends who kept cropping up as a potential suitor – something Peter denied – as was former *I'm A Celebrity...* winner Kerry Katona.

The public seemed to be transfixed on Peter and Kerry being an item and this was probably in no small part due to the fact that Katie was something of a rival to her former jungle campmate, after the two blondes seemed to be constantly at each other's throats. But rumours of Peter dating the mum-of-four just wouldn't go away after Kerry went to see the singer in concert two nights in one week. They were also purported to be 'in love' after sharing a string of romantic meals out together.

Publicly they also sang each other's praises in interviews, with Kerry saying she was 'Team Pete' and he was 'perfect boyfriend material', while he praised the ex-Atomic Kitten star with being a good mum despite her recent drug shame. The TV stars, who shared the same management team, had remained in touch after appearing on *I'm A Celebrity*... in 2004 and had always remained supportive of each other throughout their respective rocky marriages.

It was easy to see why people wanted Peter and Kerry together – lost souls united, they were two single parents who had been badly hurt in their marital break-downs and could gain strength from each other. But Peter was adamant nothing had developed beyond friendship and was keen on setting the record straight.

'There was a story saying Kerry and myself are in love. She actually said she loves me as a friend and that was said a long time ago,' he told *New!* magazine. 'We have been mates for a long time, but since she has signed to my management, I have seen her twice. She came along to two gigs, but we have not been out for cosy dinners and we are definitely not a couple. There is absolutely no way in the world I would cross that line with Kerry.

'For those of you who are interested, I can confirm that I am still single but that I am very much back on the dating scene. But I won't be telling you anything until I've met someone I'm serious about.'

Despite the denials, rumours continued to swirl about their continued friendship and it was clearly irritating Katie, even though she was adamant, perhaps *too* adamant, she didn't care.

'The whole Peter/Kerry thing really does not worry me whatsoever,' she wrote in her blog. 'I have moved on like you would not believe, I think you all know that now and the papers can carry on writing what they want.'

To be fair, recently-single Kerry didn't help matters by claiming a psychic had told her shortly after splitting from second husband, Mark Croft, that her next lover would be a 'guy in the business with a name beginning with "P"'. No prizes for guessing who she meant, but Peter nipped that speculation in the bud too.

'I can't wait for Kerry to marry her Paul or her Patrick,' he told the *Daily Star*. 'It's a shame I don't have any friends with a P initial.'

Eventually the stories about Kerry disappeared after being replaced by something of a scandal – QVC presenter Lee Clark accused Peter of destroying his marriage. He claimed the singer had sent hundreds of 'saucy' text messages to his wife, Channel 5 host Pollyanna Woodward, and threatened to name Peter in his divorce papers.

It was clearly just what the press had been waiting for – the squeaky clean, family man image he'd maintained since his divorce was falling apart at the seams – and the story about the alleged affair was being churned out across a host of newspapers and magazines. Peter was livid; it had been blown vastly out of proportion and clearly there had been something of a communication breakdown between husband and wife with him stuck squarely in the middle.

Heartbroken Lee had ranted: 'This marriage was perfect until he started texting my wife. We were blissfully happy but then he turned her head and her heart.'

Peter had met the pretty *Gadget Show* presenter at a launch party and after exchanging numbers invited her as a guest to his show in Birmingham – along with her niece. Afterwards, the pretty TV host publicly contacted Peter on his Twitter page, saying how much they had enjoyed the evening, but her husband said it didn't stop there. He claimed hundreds of text messages between the two followed, as well as email confirmations that Polly had sent him chocolates and bought sexy underwear.

One text Peter was supposed to have sent read: 'I'm lying in my 8ft bed alone. Bored. Wish you were here', to which Polly replied: 'I'm lying in my 6ft babe, alone too.'

Peter was subsequently called by Lee, who wanted an explanation and the singer did everything to allay his fears.

'He was very charming and called me "Buddy",' Lee said. 'Peter said that the relationship was purely platonic and he would put an end to it.'

Pollyanna spoke out in defence of Peter too and said they had never had a relationship but the reasons for her divorce were 'personal issues' between herself and TV presenter Lee.

'They've never so much as kissed or held hands. All he did was exchange some texts with a woman who said she was single. As soon as he found out she was married, he ended the friendship and changed his number,' Peter's management replied.

It had definitely been an unpleasant saga but thankfully the story was quickly forgotten and besides, unbeknownst to the public, he was already deeply embroiled in a new relationship. And this time, he was convinced he'd found Mrs Right.

Mum-of-two Elen Rivas, the ex-wife of footballer Frank Lampard, was introduced to Peter a month before his arena tour at his manager Claire Powell's birthday dinner party. The pair hit it off straightaway and for almost three months managed to keep their love affair secret.

Peter had managed to do a great cover-up story by continually talking about being single and what his ideal woman might look like: 'I'm more into legs and bums, but I've changed as I've got older. Now I look at a girl and think: "Is she good with kids? Can she cook? Is she kind?"' he said at the time.

Stunning Spanish-born Elen certainly fitted the bill. She was a devoted mother, had a large circle of supportive friends and was a self-confessed 'foodie'. Once their relationship was out in the open, she revealed: 'I love food. Pete can't believe how much I eat when we go out. I have bigger dinners than him.'

Her ideal partner also sounded like Peter for she

admitted in an interview a few months before they met: 'My dream man must be funny, tall, olive-skinned, intelligent and fit. They don't need to be rich – I'm doing okay and I will never date another footballer as long as I live!'

On realising that Elen was serious relationship material, Peter eventually made no secret of their love affair. But on going public, the singer was accused of having a 'show-mance', with cynics claiming their shared management team simply put them together because they wanted to create the next celebrity power couple.

'It was the opposite, I'd never even heard of her before,' Peter said of the rumours. 'My manager told me who she was signing, but I thought she said "Helen Rivers" and took a guess that she was some relation to Joan Rivers and expected to meet an old lady! Also, neither I nor my management would be part of a stunt like that, we just wouldn't do it. And we never went to parties or premieres with that in mind – I just don't get it.

'She introduced herself in her sexy Spanish accent and I thought: "This girl is too good to be true." She's so gorgeous, sexy and stunning.'

Before long the loved-up couple were seen enjoying a string of dates, including a meal out at London hotel Claridges before going on to a West End show, while Peter turned out to support Elen as she battled it out as a contestant on ITV's *Dancing On Ice*.

As well as being family-orientated the pair spent hours in the gym together, where Peter helped her train for the show by teaching her boxing and bodybuilding skills. He even introduced his children, Junior and Princess, to Elen's two daughters, Luna and Isla – then five and three – over the Christmas holidays and he told friends things had turned 'serious'.

After leaving Elen's 36th birthday party at a trendy London restaurant with friends, four months after first meeting, Peter was clearly smitten, telling waiting paparazzi: 'The right one comes along if you're patient.' But while the couple had made no secret of their relationship, it wasn't developing as fast as the whispers of marriage and shared houses were making out.

Elen wrote on the social networking site Twitter: 'How funny, Mr A and I just been told that online it says we gonna marry n moving in together.

'It's flattering to c how people have the time to write things about us. It'll be nicer to read the truth though. Lol xxxx'

Speaking about her party, she Tweeted: 'We had an amazing night, the ones we're [sic] always remember.'

Peter's life was looking increasingly settled, even his relationship with Katie was remarkably easy going, which – one could argue – was because she had recently dumped her husband Alex and was looking for all the support she could get.

'There was a story about me bumping into my ex-wife while we were both doing some Christmas shopping. This is true and I'm happy to say that it was all very civil,' he joked in his column.

Katie was in a bit of a mess and now happily ensconced in a positive and nurturing relationship, a self-confident

Peter didn't seem to mind helping out the mother of his children in her hour of need. Her 11-month marriage to Alex had been rocky for some time. As with Peter, they had started to publicly snipe at each other, and as well as putting the cage fighter down professionally, Katie didn't seem to like the fact Alex was getting more TV work either.

As well as rumours of furious rows and sex bans, they had started to lead completely separate lives with Katie attending promotional and charity events while Alex trained for fights and attended acting lessons.

Alex's camp also claimed Katie had never got over Peter and her decision to dump her husband once and for all was in direct response to her ex's romance with Elen. Katie herself later admitted Alex had been a 'rebound' and Peter was completely unsurprised by the latest turn of events in his ex-wife's life.

'Pete always knew the relationship happened far too quickly and it would end in a disastrous divorce,' a friend told the *People* newspaper. 'His main concern is that the children will have to see their mum go through a tough time and it's going to affect them.

'Despite what's gone on in the past he still genuinely wants Katie to be happy.'

As Katie moved out of the marital home and into her mum's house for some space as she prepared to serve her divorce papers, Peter helped pick up the pieces by being at the end of the phone as she texted and called him for advice.

Ever the family man, the singer was no stranger to putting aside differences in times of trauma and it was clearly taking its toll on Katie – which in turn could have serious repercussions on his children.

'Peter and Katie have been speaking, which is a good thing in itself,' a friend revealed. 'Pete made it clear he was there to help out with the kids while she goes through the break-up from Alex. The truth is he thinks she should never have got into a relationship with him in the first place.'

That may well have been true but as always, Katie was a law unto herself. The brief period of civility turned out to be the calm before the storm and it wasn't long before they were once again embroiled in arguments, which seemed to be as vicious as ever before. The first war of words came after Katie took little Princess to a hair salon in London's Soho to have her corkscrew curls flattened poker-straight.

Livid, Peter wrote in his *New!* column: 'A three-year-old shouldn't have her hair straightened. If she wants to do it when she's older, that's fine.'

He became further infuriated when after a skiing holiday in Klosters, Switzerland with Katie, his daughter returned with a nasty burn under her armpit from being in a sauna.

Peter discovered the injury – described by a newspaper who had seen a photo as 'five or six centimetres long, dark red, ridged, blistered and scabbed' – and tried to get hold of Katie for an explanation. When that failed, he contacted his lawyers to get answers.

The story was leaked to the press and Katie retaliated by accusing Peter of spilling the beans to garner publicity. She also said Junior and Princess would no longer be appearing in her TV show or making press appearances and asked Peter to do the same.

In a statement on her website, she wrote: 'Princess has in fact got a minor burn under her armpit that she received in a fluke accident when she was in Klosters. At that time she was with my mother and sister and had (unbeknown to my sister) followed my sister to retrieve pyjamas left to warm.

'That injury was seen to immediately and while it is of course upsetting that it happened at all, it was an accident of the type that happen to children all the time. Princess is fine, there will be no lasting damage and she was and is in no discomfort.

'At a time when I am trying to persuade my ex-husband to remove the children from the public eye to have this incident appear in the press and garner a little publicity is quite shameful.'

Clearly incensed, Katie then took to Twitter to point out that her eldest son Harvey had been scalded in the bath while in Pete's care a few years previously.

She wrote: 'Again lies being reported! As for peter he should know what a real BURN is like look at HARVEYS leg that he burnt while in PETES CARE!! (sic)'

The tit-for-tat rows were getting more and more frequent and while Peter hated being drawn into them, he again had no choice but to defend himself.

'I will not be accused of using an accident to gain publicity by Kate,' he declared in a statement. 'For the record, no one had contacted me to tell me my daughter had hurt herself. I tried to contact Kate to find out what had happened, but she didn't respond. Kate finally called. She then said I was making a big issue out of it.'

After the police were called in to investigate following a

tip-off, Katie was given the all-clear and life should have moved on. Except – of course – it didn't.

Behind the scenes, the arguments between Peter and his ex-wife seemed to be getting worse. During one furious row over Princess's burn, Katie lost her temper like never before. In a hate-filled rant over the phone, which was captured by cameras filming Peter's reality TV show, she told him: 'Look Pete, you've destroyed my life, you've made me completely unhappy. I honestly wish you would get in your car, drive as fast as you can and have a crash and die! I want you out of my life. I want you completely gone!'

Katie's spokesperson later apologised in a statement saying she wasn't aware of the recording, adding: 'Of course she doesn't really wish Peter any physical harm – but she feels it's time he stopped constantly slagging her off and considers how that might impact on their children.'

But the arguments kept coming, with Peter also being accused of being 'pure evil' by his ex-wife, who believed he was still in love with her.

'If you knew what went on over on Peter's side of things, it's pure evil,' she said in an interview in which she also admitted to still sleeping with her ex-husband Alex, despite their impending divorce.

'He's probably still f*****g in love with me,' she added, 'That's the problem. There's a thin line between love and hate.'

The public slanging match was incessant, but thankfully there was some respite on the horizon. Peter's parents, Savva and Thea, were coming over to the UK to spend time with their grandchildren and Junior and Princess had been learning Greek for the occasion. The singer also decided to take the pair to Dubai for a half-term holiday to get away from all the negative publicity. It was just the sort of break and return to stability they needed – especially with the next saga round the corner for Katie was about to fall head over heels for a new man. As Peter spent quality time with the children, his ex-wife jetted off to America for a photo shoot and was snapped drunkenly flirting with men and women at Elton John's post-Oscars party.

After apparently causing a scene after 'slurring her words and trying desperately to kiss any man who would listen', Katie left the bash in the early hours with 25-year-old Argentinian model Leandro Penna. The following morning, the mum-of three tweeted a photo of them both in the back of a cab together and, it seemed, Katie didn't look back. A fortnight later, she brought her toyboy hunk, branded a 'Peter Andre look-a-like', back to Britain and had reportedly asked him to marry her.

'It's a match made in heaven,' a 'friend' of Leandro's told the *Sun*. 'He's a bit of a male bimbo – a himbo. He's a model, TV star and wannabe actor, better known for his looks than for his talent.'

It was clear Peter's ex was falling for this new man fast. Not only was she posting photos of him over the internet, declaring her love for him and joking they couldn't speak the same language – Leandro had also been snapped with Peter's children.

It was history repeating itself, except the new father figure was no longer Alex but an even younger version who

Peter had never met and knew very little about. Leandro was photographed cradling Junior on a family day out at an *X Factor* meet and greet at London's O2 Arena, standing alongside Katie and Princess.

Although clearly unhappy with the situation, Peter remained tight-lipped while friends branded it a publicity stunt.

'Of course it's upsetting seeing Junior draped around her latest flame but it's not really a surprise. Going to an *X Factor* event isn't the sort of thing a celebrity like Kate can do without being spotted,' the pal said. 'This is a blatant publicity stunt. She did the same thing with Alex Reid a couple of years back.'

Of course there was very little Peter could do about it and kicking off about Katie's choice of men would have done more harm than good, especially since the children seemed happy with the arrangement.

In any case, Peter had his own love life to take care of – and his relationship with Elen appeared to have taken a turn for the worse. Whispers had already circulated it was coming to an end after the pair had both arrived and left separately at a cafe launch hosted by their mutual friend, Danielle Brown. Peter had also been spotted in a reported romantic clinch with *The Only Way Is Essex* star Amy Childs at a nightclub and although this turned out to be nothing more than an intimate conversation, it was further proof that they were spending time apart.

A few weeks later, Peter admitted they had gone their separate ways and unlike his past acrimonious splits, the singer managed to avoid a public fall-out. They had made a pact at the start of their five-month relationship to be honest and open with each other in the event of a break-up and said they would always remain friends.

'I made a promise to Elen in secret before we started dating. I said whatever happens to us, if it doesn't work out we will revert to being friends. That was our agreement,' he explained afterwards.

'When problems did start, it was because of our busy schedules and we suddenly stopped seeing each other. So before anyone could get hurt we made that decision to be friends. We honestly are.'

Another reason for the split was that Peter and Elen had both decided not to tell the children about their romance so as not to complicate things, with the result being that they rarely spent any intimate time together.

'We never spent any time on our own. It's partly our own fault because we were both so keen to protect our kids that if we spent family time together, we'd always have other people around.

'Then I was working, she was working. We'd spend a night together once a month. That was never going to work. I still think she's an amazing, beautiful classy woman and there's still a massive sexual attraction between us. But it was never going to go anywhere and we're better off as friends.'

Peter did indeed stay in touch and the pair were seen enjoying a coffee out together, while Elen helped organise Harvey's 9th birthday party.

'I've decided I'm going to throw them a party. I'm going to organise it myself, but as the lovely Elen Rivas is great at organising kids' parties, I think I'll ask her to give me a helping hand,' he said after their split.

The singer was back to adjusting to life as a single Dad but as a hot bachelor he was also keen to put himself back on the market. Peter hosted lads' nights out with his brothers Michael and Danny and celebrity pals Joe Swash, Gino D'Acampo and Keith Lemon, while being wary of the inevitable – and unavoidable – female attention.

'It's a bit scary because a girl can come up to me and innocently ask for a picture, then sell it to the papers and do a kiss-and-tell. Then I have to defend it and that's a hassle,' he explained. 'But when it's genuine with the girls, I usually like to take the party back home. Without the cameras...'

It's not as if Peter needed any extra focus on his love life for the rumour mills were churning out name after name of famous women he was supposedly bedding.

I'm a Celebrity... sweetheart Stacey Solomon was one such girl in the frame after they had been seen out clubbing together. But again, it was just more speculation.

'I wish!' Peter sighed. 'But Stacey has a boyfriend. She's gorgeous and hilarious and I wish I could say something is going on, but there isn't. She calls me a crazy geek and I call her a geek. We go out and have a massive laugh together. She's the best.'

In truth, Peter was still on the lookout for the right woman and while Katie's relationship was becoming ever more serious with Leandro as she met his family in Argentina, the singer was back to square one – and loving it.

'I'm a massively passionate person. A dirty little rotter in the bedroom and a gentleman too. The whole package, I hope. It's time to live dangerously and have fun!' he declared.

But now older and wiser, and with plenty of experience behind him, Peter also knew he didn't need a relationship to make him happy and he was content in so many other aspects of his life.

His singing career showed no signs of slowing down with a European tour in the pipeline, his new perfume 'Mysterious' was flying off the shelves and he had a new ITV show called *Here 2 Help*.

The premise of the show was for Peter to each week help someone in need but instead of being armed with a budget, the TV star had to trade his own services to get the goods he needed to make dreams come true.

Peter's TV career was now doing exceptionally well and a fourth series of *The Next Chapter* was scoring double the audience figures of his ex-wife's. On the opening episode, it pulled in over 800,000 viewers – despite being scheduled on the evening before Prince William's much-hyped marriage to Kate Middleton – while Katie's show attracted only 410,000.

'Peter is over the moon with his ratings. He didn't expect anybody to watch it as it was the night before the Royal Wedding and there was so much great television on that night,' a close friend revealed. 'He is very happy and glad that people are still interested in what he is up to.'

It was clear that Peter wasn't failing in the popularity stakes and as well as being crowned Celebrity Dad Of The Year for the second consecutive year, his fans seemed to be growing year-on-year too. Not only that, he was attracting a more mature audience and he noticed on his arena tour that it wasn't just girls in their 20s throwing their underwear at him.

'When I first started out, I had teenage girls throwing their knickers at me,' he said at the time. 'Now my fans range from nine to 90, which is great, but someone did throw a big pair of bloomers in my face, which was a new experience. The owner had pretty much written an essay on them to say how much she loved me.'

Peter was riding the crest of a wave in pretty much all areas of his life – but his love life was something he needed to work on. He had realised that no sooner had he found someone that he wanted to settle down with than he wanted to back off. Not only did he have a few commitment issues, leading such a busy life as a singer, TV star and Dad meant he was happy these days to swap nights out meeting people for relaxing evenings at home in front of the TV.

'I've started watching fishing programmes on the Discovery Channel with my mate Carl on a Friday night,' he moaned, 'I'm getting sad and old. I used to look in the mirror and think I looked pretty cool, but that changes as you get older.

'It's weird I can get everything right work-wise. I've got the family life and I feel good. But love life, it's just a bit all over the place. I don't want to be single but then I meet someone and [if] it starts getting too close, I sort of back off.'

For now, he was to concentrate on everything he was

good at and leave love to chance. He would have no shortage of offers though and in a bizarre twist of fate even his ex-wife Katie was to ask him for another shot at their marriage. Everyone, it seemed, wanted a little piece of Pete.

CHAPTER THIRTEEN

WAKE UP AND SMELL THE COFFEE

It was time to spend some quality time with the family. Peter was desperate for Junior and Princess to spend the summer of 2011 hanging out with his parents, Savva and Thea, and so they all jetted off to the Costa Del Sol for a big family reunion in a rented villa.

With so many cherished childhood memories of his parents – being taught to cook family recipes by his mum and fishing with his dad near their beachside home in Australia – Peter knew his children would benefit from spending time with the close-knit and seemingly-unbreakable Andrea family whenever possible. But after a week of fun in the sun, his elderly father Savva fell desperately ill and was rushed to hospital.

Respecting his parents' wishes, Peter refused to divulge what had happened but confirmed his father had had to undergo an operation. Despite this unexpected turn of events, the Andrea family – as always – pulled together to make the best out of the situation.

'We were all having a great time but our trip took a turn for the worse and my Dad got really ill. He was admitted to hospital and he's still there now, poor thing,' Peter wrote in his *New!* column the following week.

'We've all been pulling together and taking it in turns to look after the kids and go and see Dad. Mum's so dedicated to him that she hasn't been coming back to the villa at night to have dinner with us as it would mean he'd be on his own. She's so sweet.'

After the op, Savva was well enough to travel but needing further treatment. Peter flew them back to the UK, where he called on his good friend and surgeon Ru MacDonagh for help. Having removed Peter's kidney stones in an emergency operation the previous year, the top doctor agreed to treat his father too.

After a second bout of surgery Peter looked after Savva as he recuperated at his East Sussex home and despite the difficult circumstances the youngest of the Andre siblings loved playing host to his nearest and dearest, especially when it was his turn to look after Harvey, Junior and Princess too. Indeed it was testament to his down-to-earth parents that despite appearing in the press more often than the Pope and Nelson Mandela had done over the past five years, Peter's home life was surprisingly normal.

'On a Friday night the kids love it when I make tuna pasta and we watch a DVD afterwards. Princess or "Pringles" as I love to call her always wants to watch [Disney movie] *Tangled*,' he revealed.

'I love making a rack of lamb with roast potatoes and lots of vegetables. But I prefer doing a barbecue, whatever the weather. The Greeks do it differently to the Brits – we have a rotisserie with chunks of meat or chicken on it.

'Normally I'd speak to my mum every weekend but they have been staying at my house while my dad recovers from his operation. They are due to go back to Oz in a few weeks and I'm going to miss them,' he added.

It was clear they were keeping him grounded and so family focused was Peter that he had buried the hatchet with Katie and even given her boyfriend Leandro his blessing. The two men had met for the first time at Junior's sports day and far from being awkward, Peter revealed it had gone surprisingly well.

'We were both there to support our son on his special day and things were perfectly amicable,' Peter wrote in his column. 'My children always come first and I would never have it any other way. Leandro seemed like a very nice man.'

The lull in the couple's feuding came at a good time since Peter had plenty to be getting on with; namely in that his music career looked as if it was experiencing something of a shaky turn. Even though his summer was filled with one-off concerts and festival appearances across the UK, Spain, Egypt and Dubai, sometimes playing to massive 15,000–capacity audiences, his single had flopped in spectacular style.

'Perfect Night', the second track from his album *Accelerate* hit the charts at No. 48 after receiving little radio airplay.

Peter had been on a non-stop publicity trail, performing it on ITV breakfast shows *Daybreak* and *This Morning*, and had taken the slightly unusual route of selling it exclusively on shopping channel QVC. But as ever, he was undeterred by the disappointing sales and keen to let the critics know that this didn't spell the end of his career.

'It's a real shame that people won't play my songs on the radio, but I'm not bitter about it as I have so many things to be grateful for.

'I've always said my kids are my fiercest critics but Junior absolutely loves "Perfect Night", so that's good enough for me.'

He also defended his new method of promotion on the shopping station, which had helped Welsh singer Charlotte Church's album *Back to Scratch* reach No. 23 in the album charts the year before. It may not have been conventional but Peter appeared on QVC every morning in the single's launch week in a bid to get it sold.

'For people who have questioned why I am appearing on QVC to promote my single "Perfect Night", why not?' he hit back at the doubters. 'Don't knock it until you've tried it! So many artists have done it and it's a new avenue of promoting music.

'Just a few months ago I sold out the O2 Arena. If I'm going to go there and 200 people turn up, then I'm going to think it's time to quit.

'Things are moving very well with my music – at the weekend I played a gig to 15,000 people and as long as that happens then I will carry on.'

Besides, singing was now just one of many strings on

Peter's bow. Not only did he have his new primetime show, *Here 2 Help* and his long-running ITV2 reality series, *The Next Chapter*, he had also been nominated for a National Television Award.

Although he was eventually pipped at the post by cult E4 hit *The Inbetweeners*, Peter had plenty more to celebrate. His newly named fly-on-the-wall series, *Peter Andre: My Life*, was hitting over one million viewers a week and he was yet again proving his popularity as a presenter, with stints backstage at *The BRIT Awards, The MOBO Awards* and *This Morning*. As far as he was concerned his TV career was coming on in leaps and bounds and although many were quick to criticise that his children were being highly exposed in being allowed to star in his show, the singer was adamant nothing was going to change.

Katie too had long been demanding the youngsters were taken off the series but Peter refused. Not only did it mean that he could work while spending quality time with his loved-ones, both Junior and Princess enjoyed being in the limelight and he was confident it wasn't damaging them in any way.

'I'll use my kids in the show as long as they're happy for it. I wish my dad had made more home videos of us when we were little, and that's how I see them – as home videos,' he said at a launch party.

There was no questioning Peter's strong paternal instincts, his children remained his No. 1 priority in everything he did. Throughout his divorce from their mother, he had tried hard to provide as much stability as possible, which included regular routines whenever they visited. One of which was reading to Junior and Princess every night before bed.

It was a picture-perfect scene often played out on his TV show so when publishing giant Ladybird Books contacted him about becoming a children's author Peter leapt at the chance. Not only did he enjoy reading to his own children, thoughts of his parents settling him in every night with a book in the bedroom of their modest London home as a boy meant that this was still one of his favourite memories.

'My parents are very devout Christians so Mum and Dad would read us Bible stories and give us prayers at night before we went to sleep,' he explained to a parenting website.

'Having a nice book read to you plays on your sub-conscious as you drift off and it's positive. That's not something you'd get from playing a computer game.

'Everyone knows how crazy I am about my kids and how I'm always reading stories to them on my TV show, so it seemed like a good idea.'

In a further tribute to his family the two paperbacks for pre-schoolers, *A New Day At School* and *A Happy Birthday Party*, featured three main characters – Peter, Debbie and Mike – named after his siblings. The first was about first-day nerves at primary school – an issue close to his heart since being in the classroom hadn't always been a happy place for Peter – while the other stemmed from his love of organising parties for his three children.

'I based it on my childhood though rather than my kids' lives, so the characters are me and my brother and sister, Michael and Debbie,' he explained.

'I decided I wanted one book to be about starting

primary school and another about celebrating a birthday, as a way of helping kids to understand new things.

'I talked through the ideas with my kids and they said they loved them.'

If that wasn't enough to keep him busy, Peter had another life-long ambition come to fruition – owning a coffee shop. Over the years he'd had many vices – exercise, booze, sex – but one of his more harmless, and perhaps greatest addiction of all, was coffee. Already he had a gym in Cyprus and being a family man through and through, he was constantly on the lookout for another opportunity to go into business with his brothers.

Taking on board his father's advice of investing in ventures outside the precarious music industry, the singer plumped on buying a small outlet in the town of East Grinstead, just a stone's throw from his home. Along with siblings Danny, Chris and Michael, the brothers launched the New York Coffee Club. Some corners of the press predictably scoffed it signalled the end of his career, with one critic saying: 'He hasn't had a number one hit for quite some time now, so Peter Andre has taken his skills elsewhere'. But Peter himself remained undeterred.

'We, the brothers, have been talking about opening a coffee shop in England for many years now,' he explained. 'We went on holiday years ago to New York and kept going back to this Starbucks – it was one of the first to open and it had this great relaxed feel to it. In Australia it is hard to get a bad coffee, yet over here it is hard to get a good one. As everybody knows coffee is our obsession, so we thought why not open our own coffee shop?'

But four months after the star-studded launch, which included an appearance from good pal and rumoured ex-lover *The Only Way Is Essex* star Amy Childs, the Andrea brothers found themselves in hot water. Health inspectors blasted the American-themed eaterie for dirty floors and overflowing bins, awarding it just one out of five stars. In a damning report from the local council, other problems included meat being thawed at room temperature and Peter, along with his brother, cafe manager Danny, was ordered to make 'urgent improvements'.

'Of course, I was horrified,' Peter said, some months later. 'I don't want that to be part of what I do. My brother Danny went straight to the inspectors, and we worked with them.

'There were a few issues involving putting in extra sinks and making changes, which we implemented straight away. They came back and we went from a score of one out of five to five out of five. That's what you do – you come back fighting, you make things better.'

Six months later he was indeed fighting back with the opening of another coffee shop in Brighton – but there was still one area of his life he needed to get 'better'. He was still no closer to finding love and settling down with a new partner.

Of course he hadn't been short of company. Throughout the summer he had enjoyed another red-hot romance with one of his backing dancers, Kristina Macmillan. The stunning brunette was part of the dance troupe on his XLR8 arena tour and they had engaged in some serious on-stage chemistry.

The pair had been friends for almost a year when the singer confirmed that the 'wonderful girl' he had discreetly talked about dating was 27-year-old Kristina.

'We have been friends for over a year and we've got on really well. Who knows what could happen,' he confided in his column.

With the relationship now out in the open, Kristina started to make more and more frequent public appearances in Peter's life. As well as being spotted in the audience of the West End show *Ghost: The Musical* when Peter appeared in a one-off performance for charity fundraiser Children In Need, Kristina also Tweeted a photo of them both in Egypt after one of his concerts, saying: 'ALWAYS A LAUGH WORKING WITH ANDRE!! HAHAHA!'

A month earlier the pair had hung out together after one of his shows in Marbella, Spain, and Kristina tweeted another photo of them smiling coyly on a night out in a local music venue.

Peter was enamoured by her, that much was obvious, but his friends maintained the relationship had always been more 'off' than 'on'.

'Pete and Kristina were seeing each other, but they're not right now. Luckily, they're still really good friends and there's no awkwardness between them. Kristina went along to support Pete when he did his bit for Children In Need in the West End,' a friend told *New!* magazine at the time.

'Pete thinks she's a beautiful girl, but it's one of those situations where they're probably better off as friends than as lovers.'

But just when he thought his ailing love life couldn't get any worse, Peter had one of the most unexpected proposals of his life. As he set off for another trip back to the Australian jungle to make a one-off appearance on *I'm A Celebrity...* the woman who had turned his head seven years previously on the hit TV show decided she wanted him back.

Initially, one might be forgiven for thinking it was Peter's ex, Angela Mogridge, who was interested in reuniting with the TV star. Peter had been lured back by the producers of the ITV1 series for a guest spot and during a break in filming he took advantage of being back in his hometown by arranging to meet old flame Angela in a nearby hotel. The pair got tongues wagging after they were seen chatting intimately in the hotel bar and to intensify rumours further, Angela told fellow guests they were 'talking business'.

'Angela and Peter have been friends for years and in many ways she is the real soulmate he met in the jungle. They keep being drawn back together,' a friend confirmed. 'Who knows what will happen? They were careful not to be pictured together, though.'

And in a repeat of 2004, when Peter was caught between the two women, Katie was back home in Britain, hinting there might be a reconciliation on the cards with the Tweet: '@mrpeterandre good luck in Oz and remember what I said.'

Peter meanwhile was making his surprise entrance into the Australian jungle to host a song-writing challenge for the new celebrity campmates – who included Fatima

Whitbread and reality TV star Mark Wright – to give them the chance to win a hot-tub party with him. It was an emotional return to the camp, but although he felt 'spooked' by returning to the spot where millions of viewers had witnessed him fall in love with Katie, he found it something of a cathartic experience too.

'There's a lot of good memories here, I have no bad memories. I always feel something when I come back to Australia,' he told the celebrity contestants. 'The fact I'm back in the place where I met my future wife I had kids with – of course you're going to feel something.

'But me and Kate, we're trying to build bridges and trying to be friends for the kids' sakes.'

Before leaving, he thanked the campmates for letting him return and revealed he would happily go back to the jungle for a charity version of the show.

It had been a major success and hot on its heels was a whirlwind of rumours that his appearance had triggered Peter and Katie to rethink their divorce.

The pair allegedly wanted to start afresh by spending Christmas and New Year as a family with a view to working out if a future together was feasible. Despite seeming acutely far-fetched to avid followers of the celebrity duo, the story actually wasn't too far off the mark. In a bizarre turn of events, Katie called Peter and asked if he wanted to give their relationship another go.

Not only had Peter moved on and was quite content leading the single life, it was strangely timed in that the weeks preceding her proposal had been hardly smooth going between the two. While Peter was in the Australian jungle, Katie had been forced to issue a grovelling apology to him in London's High Court for alleging he cheated on her.

The singer had brought defamation proceedings against his ex-wife after she made a string of outrageous claims to celebrity magazine *Heat* and while recording her appearance on *The Graham Norton Show*.

As well as accusing Peter of having an affair with his manager Claire Powell – to whom she paid damages the previous year for the same claim – Katie also said in an interview that her ex-husband didn't love her son Harvey like he said he did.

After agreeing to pay Peter's £200,000 legal bill, Katie's solicitor said: 'Ms Price regrets making the comments she made and she is very happy to confirm – as she has said publicly before – that Mr Andre has been a good father to Harvey and has demonstrated his love for him on many occasions.'

While Peter's lawyer remarked that the singer now 'wanted to put the matter behind him', Katie's next attempt at smoothing over their troubled past brought a whole new scenario to their already complicated relationship.

Admittedly she had broken up with Leandro Penna several months previously and was more vulnerable than ever when single, but even so asking Peter to take her back came as a surprise to everyone. Some even speculated that the latest development was all part of a massive publicity stunt and that they had always planned to get back together at some point down the line.

'She did 100 per cent ask me to get back with her

romantically. She wanted us to spend Christmas and New Year together, but I won't ever go there,' Peter revealed.

As far as he was concerned, too much had been said and done, and he was certain he could never rekindle their relationship in that sense. He was however prepared to give their friendship another shot and invited Kate to spend some time at his house when she arrived to pick the children up on Christmas Day. Perhaps predictably, it didn't quite work out as planned.

'I didn't spend Christmas Day with Katie, as was suggested – I saw her for about half an hour for a cup of tea and I offered her some food,' he explained. 'I had all the family and some friends there, and afterwards she said I'd made her feel awkward.

'I find that upsetting because I did suggest she sent someone else to pick the kids up to avoid any trouble, but she was adamant.

'At the time I thought it had been a step forward in us being amicable. It's draining and I feel like I can't win.'

Katie didn't deny it either but took to her blog to explain there had been times when she wanted to get back with Peter for the sake of the children, but he had long made it clear that there was no chance of a reconciliation.

The singer was livid about the accusation and with their tit-for-tat arguments back in full swing the pair once more resorted to speaking through lawyers.

It started to look as if Katie's desire to reunite with Peter had come to a swift end after it emerged that Leandro had turned up at her house on Christmas Day to propose. A week later, the former lovers were spotted out clubbing together in London and the relationship was clearly back on.

Peter, mind you, quite clearly couldn't have cared less: as long as she was happy, he could get on with his own life, trouble-free. And for now, while he maintained that he still loved Katie as the mother of his children, he was now focused on finding the real true love of his life.

'I started this year so positively and I want that to continue,' he told the *Daily Mirror*. 'But it will be with someone else – that's what I want from this year.'

And 2012 would indeed be Peter's year for finding true love but it also signalled the saddest year in his life to date. He was to enjoy some massive highs while being dealt some devastating blows – a new album, a huge tour, a new girlfriend and one very sick brother. There had been some tough years in Peter's life but this was, without a doubt, to be his toughest one yet.

CHAPTER FOURTEEN

A BROTHER
IN NEED

The year started out well enough. Peter had been hailed as one of the most successful stars in ITV's history and his hit reality show was signed up in an incredible two-series deal. With over two million viewers now tuning in to see the doting dad's daily escapades, he felt incredibly lucky to be able to do a job that he loved so much, even though he knew the round-the-clock exposure wouldn't be everyone's cup of tea.

'Yup, I live in a goldfish bowl! It's a pretty awesome goldfish bowl, though. My life is incredible – I have an incredible family, my kids are incredible. I've got three children, all completely different personalities, and I have all that in my life. So my goldfish bowl is pretty cool. Yes, people look in the glass, but so what?' he told TV host Piers Morgan.

'If I wanted to get away from it all, I'd just get on a plane and go somewhere. In Kazakhstan they have no idea who Peter Andre is...'

Peter's life had always been something of a rollercoaster but it had been running pretty smoothly for quite some time now. Realising how privileged he was and wanting to give something back to those who had helped him, when his good friend Dr Ru MacDonagh asked him to get involved in a charity trip to Africa, Peter jumped at the chance.

The surgeon, who had not only operated on Peter's kidney stones but had also treated his father Savva the previous year, was going to Zanzibar, an island off the coast of Africa, to raise awareness of his charity HIPZ – Health Improvement Project Zanzibar.

'He was the doctor who operated on me when I was having problems. Every time I went to the bathroom I was peeing blood, not urine but every doctor I went to couldn't tell me what was wrong.

'God knows what would have happened to me if Dr Ru hadn't found the kidney stone and rushed me in for surgery. I was collapsing and blanking out constantly and waking up screaming in pain, so Dr Ru is like a hero to me and my family,' Peter explained. 'I asked him how I could re-pay him and he mentioned HIPZ. I wanted to give something back.'

As the chairman of the charity, Dr Ru realised that Peter Andre, along with the cameras for his reality TV show, could raise crucial awareness of the small island where disease and poverty were rife and medical care was needed in abundance. The trip proved life changing, not only because Peter saw a whole new world of positivity amid such poverty but because the top surgeon's stunning daughter Emily also joined the mission.

In the not too distant future, the pretty trainee doctor would be the singer's 'dream woman' before becoming the one he wanted to spend the rest of his life with, but for now their shared experience was simply drawing them closer together. As they visited orphanages and met sick patients in local hospitals, Peter's whole perspective on life changed. For the first time ever he saw death close up when on a hospital visit three tiny children died in front of him, an experience that would haunt him forever.

'The first day I was there I saw three babies die in front of my eyes. It was the most heart-wrenching thing I've ever seen. There was a baby on oxygen and on a drip, and the surgeons were fighting to save her but she passed away in front of me.

'Just as I was about to sit down in shock I looked over and put my hand down and touched a baby that had been dead for about an hour, lying there wrapped in a blanket. I have never seen anything like it in my life. I was tortured and horrified – I can't even explain it.

'That was the worst thing I'd ever seen. Dr Ru has already worked wonders out there and I hope to help him turn things around completely.

'When you see people over there and how they suffer it changed my whole outlook on my life and massively put things into perspective.'

As well as filming some of the scenes for his new series, *Peter Andre: My Life*, the singer also kept fans up to date with his experiences on an almost daily basis.

'Here I am in Zanzibar working with my friend Dr Ru,' he wrote in his weekly magazine column alongside a photo of him with four children outside an orphanage. 'We WILL make a difference.'

He also posted a picture of himself in a hospital on his Twitter account, saying: 'One of the many malaria infected children I have met in Zanzibar with @DrRuMac. Emotional but incredibly rewarding.'

And true to the saying, 'Don't look for love and love will find you', he was so blown away by what he was witnessing in Zanzibar, romance was the last thing on his mind – even though the mutual affection between himself and Emily was clearly growing.

'Emily's an incredibly special person,' he penned in his column. 'She knows I think so highly of her. We're going to be friends for life and do you know what else? She just happens to be a bit of a hottie as well!'

While nothing had happened between them, in between witnessing the tragic scenes in Zanzibar, the couple also enjoyed some hilarious and heart-warming moments together off-camera.

Ever charming and amiable, Peter had been welcomed with open arms by some of the locals and in what might have been a hint of things to come they hosted a traditional 'marriage' ceremony for him and Emily, after wrongly assuming they were a couple. But far from being awkward, so far-fetched seemed the idea that they could become Mr and Mrs Andre it became something of a joke within Emily's family that the pair were now husband and wife.

'When I was in Zanzibar with Emily and her parents, the locals thought we were a couple so they threw a "marriage" ceremony for us,' Peter revealed later that year. 'It was just a bit of fun as we weren't even together back then.

'We laughed about the fact that people thought we were and it became a running joke amongst her family that we were married.'

Even if a romance with the pretty brunette had been even a fleeting consideration at that point, it was pushed firmly to the back of Peter's mind on flying back to Britain. Like a bolt from the blue he was plunged from one life-changing experience into another when a phone call from his eldest brother back in Australia brought horrifying news.

At just 54 years old Andrew had been diagnosed with kidney cancer.

After dropping the children off with Katie, the singer, along with sibling Michael, immediately jumped on a plane to make the 24-hour journey back to his homeland to be by his brother's side.

'As soon as he told me, I got on a flight. Even though I'd just got back from Zanzibar, I didn't even think about it: family comes first.'

Restaurant manager Andrew was living with his wife Magda and teenage daughter Thea in the Gold Coast area of Australia, where Peter and his siblings had grown up. After being struck down with a mystery stomach ache, he was sent for a scan at his local hospital, where it was revealed to be cancer.

It meant having two life-saving operations to remove the disease and, concerned it could be quite advanced, doctors warned that if it had spread then it could be fatal.

'Andrew is seriously ill,' a friend confirmed. 'While the doctors have acted quickly by locating the cancer and making plans to operate, nothing is being taken for granted. It's a very tense time indeed.'

The whole family was rallying round and trying to put on a brave face for Andrew's sake but beneath the infectious Andrea smiles, they were all in a state of shock. Peter had never experienced someone so close having cancer and seeing the older sibling he had always looked up to lying helpless in hospital knocked him for six.

After two bouts of surgery, which included removing one of Andrew's kidneys, the family faced a terrifying wait to see if he had been cured or if the disease had spread to other parts of his body.

A week into treatment, Peter admitted he was trying hard to be a rock for Andrew while supporting his elderly parents, who were distraught at being told they might lose their eldest son.

'It's been a horrific week; it's torn me apart. I've had to see my brother lie there with all sorts of medication and sleeping for hours on end. We've never had cancer in our family so it's been a very difficult time for us all. My parents are in an awful state.

'Andrew's had two massive operations to remove his kidney and then to see if it's spread. We're still waiting for the full test results but if it has spread, he's in serious trouble.

'It's been a pretty hard few weeks – the most important weeks of my life,' he revealed.

But sadly they didn't get the news they'd hoped for. Test results confirmed Andrew had stage IV cancer and was much worse than originally feared. It had spread to his stomach and lymph nodes, and he now had to undergo debilitating chemotherapy sessions.

'It was the outcome we were all dreading. We're trying hard to stay positive but it's really knocked us and if I'm honest, I'm not dealing with it very well,' Peter wrote in his *New!* column after returning home a week later.

'I don't mind admitting there's been quite a few tears on my part. But it doesn't matter how I feel, I just care about how Andrew feels. When someone in my family suffers, we all suffer. It's so hard to see a sibling go through something so awful.'

Andrew was still in hospital recovering, having good days when he could get out of bed and then relapses when he slept for hours. Peter tried to cheer him up by allowing his two children, Junior and Princess, to call him on his mobile phone. They had been told Uncle Andrew was ill but they were not told the devastating reason behind his hospital stay.

'Junior has been speaking to Andrew and he keeps asking him if he has been bitten by a snake as that's what he associates with Australia, which has made Andrew laugh.'

Peter was also trying to get his head round the fact doctors had told them it was terminal and there was no cure. Desperate to help in any way he could, the singer decided his brother's best chance of survival was to be flown to Britain for a second opinion at London's prestigious Royal Marsden hospital, which specialises in cancer treatment.

Andrew and his wife Magda made the 24-hour journey

over to the UK and moved into Peter's home, where along with his siblings, Mike, Danny and Chris, they could provide him with round-the-clock care. The treatment was going to be costly and in a gesture of how much Andrew meant to him, Peter sold his beloved Ferrari to go towards paying for it.

'Andrew is such a good guy – one of the kindest I know. We've always been close and I've always looked up to him. He doesn't deserve this as he's so healthy and really looks after himself. Then again, who does?

'What with my trip to Zanzibar and now this, I've realised you only live once and should appreciate every day,' said Peter.

'I'm determined Andrew's going to get better. If I have any power to help my family I will, because my family is the most important thing in my life.

'I decided that I wanted to bring him over to England because I knew the Royal Marsden hospital could give him the best treatment. I knew it would be tough on my parents who are in their eighties and I knew this was something I could do to help. I brought him and his wife Magda over, and they now live with me.'

Doctors at the top London hospital seemed to be more positive about Andrew's chances and along with more chemo, put him on a trial drug.

'Andrew's doing well. I'm not going to lie, it's been a struggle. We've had really tough moments, but we've also had good ones,' Peter revealed a few weeks into treatment.

The Andrea family were closer than ever before and pulling together meant Andrew was recuperating well, with his siblings cooking him nutritious meals while Peter's son Junior kept him entertained by challenging him to games on the Xbox.

Peter too was receiving an incredible amount of support from the public as well as his celebrity friends, including Kerry Katona, Amy Childs and chef Gino D'Acampo, who all offered to help in whatever way they could. Even Bee Gee Robin Gibb's wife Dwina, whose famous husband was also fighting colon cancer, called Peter to sympathise as she too was helping a loved one through a harrowing time.

Although much of the focus was now on Peter's personal life, the singer still had work to do and taking some respite from his brother's illness there was a raft of new projects in the pipeline to focus on.

'I love my job but I'm now expanding as a businessman and also into more rewarding work,' Peter explained in an interview about his future. 'I'm going to get to a point where I will be much happier doing projects like Zanzibar. I think you just realise what is important in life. I'll never give up totally, though. My fans are too important to me. I've got lots of projects so it definitely won't be too soon. I'm talking maybe in my fifties that I might be winding down.'

Using his celebrity status to his advantage, the singer wanted to focus more on his volunteer work and was keen to add a cancer charity to the worthy causes he already fronted, including the NSPCC and the Caudwell Children's Trust. And with his TV career now firmly secured with ITV, the singer was also keen to get his music back on track.

Not only did he have millions of fans to please but with the added responsibility of paying for Andrew's private hospital treatment, it was essential he worked as much as possible.

Almost 20 years since his first album, Peter was signed up with a new record label, UK-based Snapper Records, and he excitedly started work on his ninth album. It was to be followed by a 31-date UK tour booked for the end of the year.

'It's going to be bigger than my last three albums,' Peter assured his fans. 'I'm going to go to L.A. to do some recording. I'm so pleased to be touring again too – it gives me the chance to get close to the British public, who have done so much for me.'

The *Up Close and Personal* tour, which culminated in a massive arena show at London's O2 for the second time in two years, was a sell-out and Peter was determined for it to live up to its name. With lots of surprises up his sleeve, he was working on making it his best show yet: 'I am using illusions and magicians. I want to be the first to do this. Let's just say, I could be sitting next to you and you wouldn't ever know it.'

Not content with just his TV and music career, as well as a sideline running a coffee shop, Peter had another venture up his sleeve in men's fashion. The singer had started designing a range of shirts and T-shirts, as well as kids clothes to be sold via an online fashion website, which would see another life ambition fulfilled. Not only that, playing on his single status, there was another ITV2 show in the making, Peter Andre's *Bad Boyfriend Club*, in which women called on the star to help kick their boyfriends back into shape.

His own love life was far from steady but it was another challenge he was happy to take on. Not only that, he hoped it would get him in the mood for finding love again. Peter had made a few attempts at dating girls since his second appearance in the jungle, but each one seemed to end in disaster.

One woman in the frame was Greek-Irish model Georgia Salpa, who Peter met for the first time on a champagne date with *OK!* magazine after they both admitted to fancying each other. Afterwards, Peter sent her several text messages asking to go on a date but he was rejected.

'She's a very pretty girl but she wasn't interested in me,' he admitted. 'Georgia is Greek and Irish, it is the ultimate combination.'

He wasn't disheartened by the rejection but Peter's optimistic attitude was getting a beating in other areas of his life and this time he was struggling to keep positive. While experiencing the stress of seeing his brother undergo tough cancer treatment, the singer had also been subjected to a torrent of abuse over the internet.

As with many celebrities, Peter had signed up to the social networking sites Facebook and Twitter, which meant he could communicate daily with millions of fans at one time. It was now part and parcel of the way he was able to stay in constant touch with those who mattered most to his career, updating them on his music and TV news, public appearances and personal views on anything and everything. But as liberating as this two-way fan club was, it was suddenly showing itself to have a much darker side.

Hiding behind fake names, website users known as 'trolls' started sending him sick messages and making vulgar claims against him and his family. Some of the most hurtful messages were accusations that he was pretending his brother was terminally ill to get publicity. There seemed to be no escape from it either. Every time Peter logged on to the online accounts, there was a risk that he would be faced with another chilling note. The build-up of fear he was now experiencing was reminiscent of the death threats he'd endured in the nineties, which had led to terrible panic attacks and ultimately the breakdown that almost spelled the end of his career. He could sense himself slipping down that path and admitted he was on the threshold of becoming depressed again.

'I could feel myself being pulled down by it, going into a depression.

'There are these people out there who just say the most horrendous things about my family, about me, and it's so awful that it does start to get inside your head and pull you down.

'I had things said that I was using my brother's cancer to further my career, terrible things I'd never repeat about my other brother Mike and my kids. As a kid I was bullied. I used to get picked on for being mixed race so I did Kung Fu when I was 14 to give me confidence to stop them.

'But in the case of these weak, pathetic people who don't even have the courage to put their real names on their evil messages, you don't even have the power to confront them.'

Peter put blocks on his Twitter and Facebook accounts and lent his celebrity status to get behind a government drive to stop internet bullying.

In the midst of all this, Andrew was still undergoing chemotherapy and it was a case of sitting out each batch of treatments to see if progress had been made.

'I'm not a superhero but I'm doing okay,' Peter's brother admitted, 'We're just trying to stay positive.'

At times that proved hard, especially when Andrew was rushed to hospital with a blood clot on his lung in an apparent relapse. The singer kept a bedside vigil until his brother had been treated and was allowed to return home.

Peter was clearly feeling the strain and with six months to go before his 40th birthday, he wanted to ensure the landmark birthday got off to a flying start. Not only did he want a big celebration in Las Vegas with five-days of hell-raising with his brothers and a few friends, he also planned to put his carefree, single days behind him.

As for the woman he was to marry and have more children with, Peter was confident she was within touching distance.

'Sometimes the person you're meant to marry is right under your nose but you don't realise it,' he conceded. And he wasn't wrong.

Two months later, in the summer of 2012, Peter was seen on a red carpet date with one Emily MacDonagh. It was a bold statement for the singer, who had been keen to keep every woman since Katie Price firmly under wraps for as long as possible before coming clean about the romance. But this time everything seemed different – the doctor's daughter was like no one else he had dated before. She wasn't a celebrity, she wasn't in the entertainment industry, and she definitely wasn't a glamour girl.

Sixteen years his junior, Emily was a medical student at Bristol University, whose only experience of Peter's life in showbiz was having pictures of him on her wall as a schoolgirl.

'Before, I felt empty. Now I feel like that gap has been filled – this is the happiest I've felt in years,' he declared a few months after their first date.

It was starting to look as if the pieces of the puzzle were falling into place after what had been one of the most difficult times in Peter's 39 years.

'Getting that phone call from Andrew was the worst moment in my life. The last year has been all about fighting for me. Fighting to give myself and my kids a future, fighting all my fears, fighting for my brother and fighting those awful faceless bullies who just try and destroy everything you do.'

Now he had his sights set on the next chapter of his life, which involved finding wife number two, producing a 'landmark' album, completing another UK tour and most importantly, fixing his brother. Could he pull it all off before his 40th birthday in just six short months' time?

The challenge was on.

CHAPTER FIFTEEN

A LOVE FOUND AND A LIFE LOST

The start of Peter's relationship with Emily MacDonagh seemed less than conventional. But then looking at the two protagonists in this particular romance, on paper they hardly seemed like the obvious couple either.

'She's a uni student – he's a divorced dad-of-two. She's just starting her life, enjoying her independence and about to embark on her medical career, Pete's already settled,' one magazine sniped. 'He comes with two children, an ex-wife and a management company that monitor his every move... and worst of all, Pete's her dad's mate.'

Peter knew there was every chance his 'toygirl' relationship would draw criticism from the cynics but believing Emily was worth the risk and out of respect for her family, he called his good friend Dr Ru to request his all-important blessing to date his daughter.

It couldn't have been any different from the start of his relationship with Katie Price, where the couple bickered their way into a romance live on TV in front of 11 million viewers. Speaking on his reality ITV2 show, Peter admitted: 'I've known Emily for ages, but she wasn't interested – she was in a relationship.

'She came and stayed over loads of times, but it was never like that, it was always with her family and as friends.

'Obviously things didn't work out with Emily's boyfriend, a bit of time went, and then I asked her. It was weird... I even actually... well...'

'He rang my dad for permission,' Emily interjected. 'He told my mum and they sat me down for a chat!'

Peter continued: 'And then I asked her, and thankfully she said yes, and it's perfect. I feel we're moving in the right direction.'

Emily had been in Peter's life for several years, was already known and loved by his three children, Harvey, Junior and Princess, and the pair had been spotted on nights out in London long before they were an item.

It was a wonder no one had put two and two together, but then the couple themselves hadn't expected to fall for each other either.

Unlike his romance with Jordan, where there was talk of marriage within 24 hours of dating, Peter was keen to take this relationship slowly, savour every minute and at the same time didn't seem to want to keep any part of it secret either.

After a first date at the London premiere of the movie *Magic Mike* at the Mayfair Hotel, they were snapped a week later at a top Thai restaurant before going on to

Ghost: The Musical in the West End, accompanied by Peter's sick brother Andrew.

Peter was clearly smitten and in the week photos of the pair appeared in the press, he took to his magazine column to explain what was going on.

'Emily's a beautiful girl, we've been on a few dates but we're continuing to get to know each other.'

'Pete thinks the world of her and her family,' his agent disclosed further. 'He is extremely cautious, they are taking it slow at the moment but get on tremendously well.'

To the outsider it may well have looked like a sugary-sweet romance with little of the wild, unbridled passion of Peter's sizzling flings of yesteryear. But while Peter was playing the perfect gentleman in wining and dining his new girlfriend, an exotic holiday to Cyprus a few weeks into dating unmistakably proved that all the right chemistry existed between them.

Not letting the criticism of their 15-year-age gap get in the way of happiness, they couldn't keep their eyes off each other as they snuggled up on a poolside sunbed together. Despite their various differences, Peter and Emily seemed perfectly suited as they spent hours in the dreamy location, laughing and joking in between affectionately kissing and wrapping their sun-kissed limbs around each other.

After his hundreds of flings, doomed relationships and a failed marriage, the star – who was clearly still a dab hand at turning on the charm – also admitted his new show, *Bad Boyfriend Club*, was helping him woo the stunning student. In it, the singer helped transform hapless boyfriends – among them a workaholic, a useless

DIY-er, a bloke obsessed with *Superman* and several who preferred playing computer games to going out – into dream partners.

'A lot of what I've learned, I've already been putting into practice with Emily,' he joked. 'I've been watching what others have been doing wrong and making sure I don't do it too. It's done me the world of good!'

Luckily for Peter, despite being in her early twenties and significantly younger than him, Emily had a mature head on her shoulders and they didn't have to try hard to make their relationship work. She was also proving to be a massive breath of fresh air. After nearly 20 years in the music business, Peter had predictably spent much of his waking hours completely absorbed in the entertainment industry, from writing music to rehearsing, to filming and planning his next venture. Many of his former girlfriends had also been involved in showbiz so as a hardworking medical student at Bristol University, when Emily did meet up with Peter – which due to the demands of her degree was usually at the weekends – she brought something new with her: a world outside his media bubble.

Not only that, with Pete finding it hard to witness his brother's painful and unpredictable cancer treatment, Emily was proving just the tonic he needed to keep him on the straight and narrow during some very dark days.

'I think it's just really refreshing to be with someone who is in a completely different world and you can actually have a conversation with. I didn't even think about the age gap, to be honest. We're not bothered by it.

'She is someone I have a lot of respect for, so when they

[the media] were saying, "Pete's toygirl", I felt bad for her family,' Pete admitted.

'She will be a qualified doctor in 16 months so she has a busy year ahead. But I can see it going somewhere. To be honest, I'm scared to say too much. There will come a time when I will say a lot more, but it's still very early and I don't want to overdo it.'

Peter didn't really need to say anything anyway; it was obvious to everyone he was falling for Emily in a major way. A few weeks after returning from Cyprus, the singer splurged thousands of pounds in whisking her away on a secret birthday trip to Venice. Although most women would be flattered to be lavished in such a way by their lovers, Emily also embraced Peter's boyish charm and shared his infectious sense of humour.

As well as being nicknamed 'Embilism' by the smitten singer, she also became subject to his endless jokes, gentle ribbing and was quickly adjusting to his lavish gestures.

'I managed to keep where we were going a secret right up until we landed as I made her look at the floor in the airport when we were checking in!' he said of the surprise trip.

'She was really chuffed and we had an absolutely amazing time together.

'The really special thing about it was that we didn't get photographed once and that really made the holiday for us. We could just do exactly what we wanted and no one paid us the slightest bit of attention. It was total bliss!'

Peter's children had also noticed a change in their father as the pair started to spend more time with each other. They had agreed to a five-day rule whereby they vowed not to be apart for longer than a working week and Emily was fast becoming part of the Andre household.

More often than not travelling from her student digs in the West Country to Peter's lavish house in East Sussex, she was looking more and more at ease in the role of girlfriend and stepmum to Peter's two children.

Appearing on his fly-on-the-wall show she chatted easily with his brothers, who were living at his home, played happily with the children and helped around the kitchen as the dad-of-two made the evening meals.

'I think doing stuff together is the basis for a really nice relationship and she's awesome,' Peter breathed. 'Emily's very good with the children too, helping them with their homework. Princess really looks up to her – they're more interested in hanging out with her than they are with me!'

It was true: Emily was a real hit with the kids, which to Peter had always been the crucial ingredient to turning a good relationship into one that could seriously last the distance. Even still, he was adamant that they kept the romantic side of their relationship secret from the children with a no-kissing rule – although his attempts were clearly not fooling anyone. The youngsters couldn't have been more enthusiastic about Emily settling down with their father for good and they had a pretty clear idea as to what was going on.

While Princess referred to Emily as 'my best friend', a grinning Junior noted on Pete's TV series: 'My dad is acting strange. He's been acting strange for the last couple of months, because he's actually in love with Emily and he wants to marry her.'

Another clear indication that they saw her as a firm part of their lives and their future together was when Junior was filmed telling his sister a bedroom story, which started: 'Once upon a time there was a small family – me, Princess, Harvey, Daddy, Mummy and Emily.'

She had slotted easily into Peter's life and if further proof of their compatibility was needed, as he worked away on his music at home, Emily kept him company by sitting at a small desk in the corner of his studio, where she diligently studied for her medical degree. Clearly every second they could spend with each other counted.

It was no surprise, therefore, that a track on his forthcoming album, *Angels and Demons*, was for her.

'"Fly Away" is all about Emily,' Peter divulged. 'That song is exactly about us.'

And the track couldn't have made his feelings any clearer – he had fallen for her hard, and he had started to admit publicly that marriage and children could be on the cards.

Emily was touched and a measure of her mutual affection came when she joined Peter in the mixing studio to hear a final version of the track. The scene was a world away from when Peter had three years previously taken his disinterested wife Katie to his studio in Los Angeles to hear *Revelation* being produced.

Whereas Katie had looked bored and disgruntled at being pulled into Peter's world of work, proud Emily was moved to tears as the tune blared out in the sound booth and afterwards admitted: 'I'm a bit biased but "Fly Away" is a lovely song, it's just my cup of tea. It's great.'

The new 12-track record, *Angels and Demons*, was

coming on in leaps and bounds and Peter was hoping this would be the landmark album to take the world by storm. It was to herald yet another change in musical direction, combining old school funk with a contemporary twist, something he had never attempted before.

Jetting between Los Angeles and London for the album, he worked with legendary writers and producers, including Nasri, known for his work with Justin Bieber and Chris Brown, as well as Jaylien Wesley, who had composed music for Akon and Cheryl Cole.

And like *Revelation*, it was another chance for Peter to use his music as an outlet for his innermost emotions and thoughts. He had made no secret of his ability to appear happy and positive to the outside world while secretly harbouring deep-seated worries and he was now at a stage in his life where he was keen to creatively express that side of his personality.

'The album is based on personal experience, not melodies. I have good days and dark days, 99 per cent of the human race do. You can put a smile on your face but when you get home, you can feel alone. It's a feeling I've had in the past. When you shut the door, the demons take over – it's a constant battle.

'I hope it will be my biggest-selling album yet.'

After years of being coerced by record labels into making commercial hits such as his most-hated single 'Insania', Peter was keen to collaborate with other artists to build his reputation within the music industry.

So Solid Crew's Lisa Maffia, who had a string of MOBO and BRIT Awards under her belt from a prestigious 12-

year career, duetted with him on the seductive track, 'X', and agreed he was finally moving in the right direction.

'It sounds like a brand new Peter. I've never heard him sing like this, it feels really old school. I think he's always wanted to do this but he's always been taken down the commercial route,' she said.

To go with the new sound – and coinciding with a new fashion range of shirts and T-shirts called 'The Alpha Range' – Peter was also experimenting with a more mature image during the album's photo shoot, with tailored suits, jackets and the classic tuxedo and bowtie.

'It's more sleek, more adult, more classic, which I hope this album is. It's a lot richer – it's not just cheesy pop shots. I'm a lot happier. It's definitely more Michael Bublé than Michael Jackson,' he conceded.

But with just a few weeks to go until the album's release, Peter had something of a dilemma on his hands.

The record label still wanted to release 'As Bad As You Are' as a single prior to the album hitting the shops but he was adamant it was the wrong decision. With little radio play, his chance of chart success would be ruined and since Peter had no guarantees that it would be broadcast over the airwaves he was about to take matters into his own hands.

After uploading a 30-second snippet of the track for his two million Facebook and Twitter followers and repackaging it as a promo for the album, the single got a staggeringly good 4,000 listens in the first hour – but even so, it wasn't enough to guarantee success.

'I posted it up on the internet and although I had

thousands of people listening to it, it's not enough to get it to the top of the charts – it needs to be heard on the radio and that's where the problem is,' he told his radio label.

'Some of the guys on the radio who have been sent the single said they loved it, they said it was much, much more what they were talking about, but I'm not taking that risk – I'm too scared.'

The label agreed and it looked like it was the right decision. On the first day of sales, the album shot into the charts at No. 12. Although Pete had appeared on TV shows *This Morning* and *Loose Women*, as well as BBC *Breakfast* to promote it, the result was quite a feat with no radio play.

'On its first day it's in at No. 12 without the backing of the radio so we've done really well. I told Mum to go out and buy five albums – I didn't expect her to go out and buy thousands!' he joked. 'If I get Top 10 that would be the fourth Top 10 in four years.'

But sadly it wasn't to be and a week later, the album had slipped further down the charts. While it wasn't the immediate success Peter had hoped for, he still believed it had a chance of being a big seller. And with the November launch of his tour just a few weeks away, it would be getting even more promotion and with it potentially more sales.

'I think it being the biggest-selling album will be a long-term plan. It did great in its first week of release and with the tour starting soon that will grow over time.

'There are great reviews on iTunes, a lot higher than I expected. It has done exceptionally well and I'm so proud.'

There had also been another setback. To Peter's astonishment and out of the blue in the countdown to the album's release, an American hip-hop artist had angrily, and very publicly, accused him of stealing his song and releasing it on the record without his permission.

Rapper Talib Kweli claimed the singer's producers had lifted his rap and illegally used it on the sentimental track, 'Fly Away', which Pete had dedicated to Emily.

Taking to Twitter and for all to see, he ranted: 'wow @mrpeterandre you just take people's verses from other songs and put them on your album? That's what hot in the streets? ok... whoever produced *Fly Away* for @mrpeterandre is a douchebag. They took my verse from another song w/out permission. It's abt to be a fun week.' [sic]

But Peter had no idea the slip-up had occurred. Angry and embarrassed, he immediately contacted his record label to apologise and remove the offending verses from the track.

'I have never been in a position like this, the record company presented me with the song "Fly Away": heard it, loved it.

'And I said, "Who's that guy rapping?" I'll be honest with you, I'd never heard him before, so I went ahead and recorded it,' he explained.

'Unbeknownst to me no one had thought to tell him that now he's on a different record label, then he went on Twitter and started having a go at me. I got battered and all these American rappers were Tweeting me saying "We take theft very seriously...", I was like, "What the f*** are you talking about?'

After publicly apologising to both Peter and Talib, the label removed the re-mastered track and it was released without the rapper's performance.

But the show had to go on and thankfully with the incident only having received modest press coverage, it managed to go largely unnoticed.

Aside from dashing to album signings across the UK, Peter's diary was heavy with unrelenting rehearsals, with an all-male team of backing dancers for the upcoming tour – and he was feeling the strain.

'Rehearsing has kicked my bum. I'm not enjoying it but I will love the tour. I am doing ten-hour days and it's torture,' he admitted.

He was now leading a much healthier lifestyle. Gone were the days when he would neck a protein shake and nibble on some fruit before going onstage, now he would quite happily eat calorie-laden food. But with his 40th birthday fast approaching, he was feeling the pressure to look after himself.

'When I was in my twenties I cut out all fats and oil, but it isn't a healthy way to live,' he said in the run-up to his tour. 'But now I'm nearing my forties, I can't look at donuts the same – I definitely have to take it a bit seriously.'

Twenty-two years after beginning his showbiz career Peter was still nervous and excited about playing gigs and in a bid to settle his nerves, he was still following a few pre-show rituals from the old days.

'I'm not superstitious but I do have a two-hour lockdown before each gig, where I'm just on my own,' he revealed. 'For the first hour I don't talk at all. I insist on absolute silence for my throat. Then in the second hour I start to warm up doing vocal exercises, push-ups and sit-ups to get my body going. I might even have a cold shower to wake myself up.'

He was excited about the gigs – there was to be a James Bond theme to the shows, an intimate performance with his brother Chris, and a lavish light and pyrotechnic display to rival all his previous sell-out tours.

But there was no hiding from the fact that he had a lot to worry about.

Halfway through a morning of radio interviews to promote his album, Peter took a heart-breaking phone call from his brother Andrew and it was very bad news. His latest operation hadn't been a success and the cancer had spread to other parts of his body. He was now fighting a losing battle and after more radiotherapy and surgery to strengthen his back, Andrew admitted the night before the launch of Peter's tour that he was going to die.

'The cancer has been re-diagnosed,' he bravely explained, 'it's in my pelvic bone. I can feel the pain, a little bit in my lungs, a little bit in my kidney. Even to brush my teeth is an effort, to have a shower is an effort, just normal things. We've now realised that I'm riddled with this. I'm stuck with cancer now for the rest of my life, as long as that is.'

With Andrew and his wife Magda still living at Peter's house, the singer had tried hard to focus on his rehearsals and album launch interspersed with some positive family time together wherever possible, but he was now close to breaking point.

'I've seen my brother go from strong – two, three jobs a day kinda guy – to hardly being able to walk. I've seen it with my own eyes. I live with it.

'He's there in my house and I love him being there, but I guess I wasn't prepared for how heart-breaking it can be.'

He added on his ITV show, which had been documenting Andrew's fight for life: 'In the last few weeks I've felt really drained, like my head's hurting. I've had people tell me that at least take comfort in that you're doing everything you can, but how can you take comfort in that?

'I feel anxiety, it's not just mine but it's my brother's life. It's nothing to do with work, nothing to do with relationships – it's a life and he's my own blood. It's a different kind of pain, I can't describe it.

'And then I see Em and the kids, and it's like a breath of fresh air. She's so pure, awesome and funny and cool, and the kids love her. I have so many good things in my life too.'

He was now relying on his girlfriend more than ever before and she was doing everything she could to try and make his life easier by being on hand whenever possible.

'I just come over and try and look after him. We have stuck to our five-day rule. We do miss each other during the week, but it makes the weekend great,' she admitted.

Doing his best to put his heartache to one side, Peter ploughed himself into work and the first night of his 31-date *Up Close and Personal* tour at Plymouth Pavilions was a massive success.

True to its name, the opening gig in the West Country

city held a special place in Peter's heart since it had been at his gig in Plymouth, two years before that he had first met Emily. After his emergency kidney operation, he had wanted to thank his surgeon, Dr MacDonagh, and he suggested giving his wife and daughter tickets to see him in concert. Now as his girlfriend, she was with him behind the scenes and propping him up as he took to the stage for a series of high-octane routines and a mix of new and classic songs.

With several space-like outfit changes, the block-buster themed show, which channelled James Bond, *Singin' in the Rain* and *Mission Impossible*, complete with magic tricks, illusions and a duet between Pete and his brother Chris, was mind-bogglingly challenging. But Peter pulled it off, every audience went wild and the applause was deafening.

Performing for his fans not only gave him a boost, but the singer was finding the shows incredibly therapeutic. Mentally and physically, the past six months had been draining but showing true strength of character, he had managed to produce an album and now a critically acclaimed tour – and going onstage was providing an excellent escape from life at home.

'The last couple of weeks I don't even know where I am half the time and the only thing that's been great is being up on that stage. It takes you away for an hour and a half, and then you go back to reality and things are all weird,' he said.

Peter was also trying hard not to be disappointed after his plan to get Andrew to attend one of his gigs was dashed when he took a turn for the worse and had to be readmitted to hospital for more radiotherapy treatment. It would have been the first time his eldest brother had seen him perform live and the singer was desperate to put on the best show possible for him.

But with this no longer an option – and one which sadly would never come to fruition – Pete started a new pre-show ritual of calling Andrew on his mobile phone to get a pep talk from his brave brother before walking out on stage.

'He tells me to go out and "knock 'em dead",' he said. 'He just gives me that push, he's such an amazing guy.'

But midway through the tour and three days after Peter's incredible sell-out concert at London's O2 Arena the singer was told Andrew had just days to live. The devastating news was broken to him just as he was preparing to go on stage at Cardiff's Motorpoint Arena. In an incredible show of strength and not wanting to disappoint thousands of fans, Peter decided to go ahead with that evening's performance but the remainder of the tour was immediately postponed.

As the rest of the family flew over from Australia to join Peter at Andrew's bedside, including their elderly parents Savva and Thea, Peter's management confirmed: 'He is in bits. This has come as a big shock. Peter loves his fans and is loath to let them down but he is sure they will understand.'

Floored by the news, the singer wrote in his *New!* column: 'It's the worst possible end to the year.' A few days later, and just a week before Christmas, the inevitable happened and Andrew passed away in the early hours of the morning with Peter and his beloved family by his side.

'Everyone was there – his wife, his daughter, Pete and their parents – the whole family,' his management explained. 'Andrew woke up, looked around at everyone to say goodbye and then fell asleep. He passed away in his sleep. It was very peaceful.

'The whole family is in shock. It has all happened so quickly. This time last year he just thought he had a tummy ache. It's terrible.'

Having never experienced the death of such a close loved one, Peter struggled to come to terms with the loss and had no idea how the grief of losing Andrew would grip him. Having rescheduled the tour, he immediately called ITV bosses to postpone the broadcast of his reality series, *Peter Andre: My Life*. It featured scenes of his dying brother and he couldn't face having the footage screened so soon after his death.

He also put on a brave face by managing to send a Tweet to fans, after being deluged with messages of support. 'My brother Andrew lost his battle with cancer in the early hours of Sunday morning. We were all with him, holding him, till his very last breath. Absolutely devastated. So I thank you all so much for your kind words and messages you've sent. I'm sure he's reading them with me... thank you again.'

Ex-wife Katie Price had also set aside their long-running feud to be one of the first to send him a message of condolence on the social networking site, as had his former girlfriend Elen Rivas and a string of celebrities, including Kerry Katona, Emma Bunton and Phillip Schofield.

'Morning darling just sent you a text,' Kerry wrote. 'I'm so sorry to hear about Andrew ... love you loads and always here for you, Kerry and kids x', while Elen tweeted: 'My thoughts are with you and the family. Lots of love xxx #RIP.'

In a rare show of solidarity during such tough circumstances, Katie wrote compassionately: 'My thoughts are with the Andre family at this difficult time xx.'

But while he was buoyed by the hundreds of messages from well-wishers, Peter was in a state of shock and friends said his health was quickly deteriorating. In the weeks following Andrew's death, Peter lost over a stone in weight and was suffering badly from insomnia.

'He's spent the last week crying himself to sleep. He went four nights in a row not sleeping and everyone was worried about him.

'He hasn't eaten properly for weeks. He struggles to finish a slice of toast in the morning and then doesn't eat all day,' a worried friend revealed.

'Peter's clearly cut up about his brother. He has barricaded Andrew's room and won't let anyone go in there. He's not joining in with family meals or doing anything with his brothers because he feels he's betraying the memory of Andrew by enjoying himself.'

But time is a good healer and after his parents and Andrew's family returned to Australia, Peter spent as much time as he could with Emily and the children to help heal the wounds. With Christmas round the corner, he focused on trying to make it as fun as possible in the circumstances.

Decorating his house with six Christmas trees,

including a pink one for Princess, the festive season was undoubtedly hard but made better with the children to keep his mind off Andrew.

'The kids have been amazing over the last few weeks. Although Christmas wasn't the same, I still made sure I got them lots of presents. They weren't with me on Christmas Day itself but I let them open them on Christmas Eve. I spoiled them rotten,' he revealed.

After spending New Year's Eve with Emily's supportive and loving family in Somerset, the pair jetted off to Courchevel in the French Alps to go skiing and 'clear our heads'.

Peter was starting to feel more positive and his efforts to try and socialise had become easier with Emily there for support.

'Things are still pretty raw, but it does help that I've got Emily by my side. I really love having her around and it helps make everything feel okay,' he admitted.

And now into the New Year it was business as usual and as well as bravely allowing the final episode of his postponed ITV2 show to be screened, Peter went back on tour to perform his rescheduled dates.

'It's going to be tough and it's come round quickly, but I really want to put on a good show for my fans and to fulfil my work commitments. I'm hoping performing will give me something to focus on.'

And there was another diversion just around the corner, courtesy of his ex-wife Katie Price.

Just one week after Peter had returned to the road and admitted 2012 had been the worst year of his life, he made the shocking discovery that the mother of his children had secretly got married – to her boyfriend of six weeks.

Babysitting their children at the time, the first he knew of it was when the news of her secret Bahamas wedding broke online.

If there was one thing that wasn't going to change in the singer's life that he could wholeheartedly depend on, it was Katie's ability to shock him time and again. Understandably, he was livid.

CHAPTER SIXTEEN
TURNING 40

One would have expected that throughout the traumatic six months that Peter was nursing his cancer-stricken brother there would have been something of a let up in the on-going battle with his ex. But her latest shock-and-awe antics of getting married to lover Kieran Hayler with just a handful of witnesses were just the tip of the iceberg.

While the previous autumn Peter had been caring for Andrew and putting the finishing touches to his album, Katie launched a £300,000 legal battle against him. In it, the former glamour girl accused him of orchestrating a 'smear campaign' against her, following their 2009 split.

Along with Peter's former manager, Claire Powell, and former friend, Jamelah Asmar, Katie claimed the trio were behind leaking explosive details about her private life to a newspaper. Papers lodged in the High Court sought damages for 'misuse of private information', which had left her suffering 'serious distress'. They referred to the story that emerged after their separation that Katie had grown close to her riding instructor, Andrew Gould, which both parties strenuously denied.

Months down the line, the threat of a full trial was still hanging over Peter's head and it seemed the chances of ever being able to enjoy a reasonable relationship with his ex were looking increasingly unlikely.

To fans of the nation's once most popular sweethearts, it was sad that after four years of marriage and two children, they still seemed to be continually at each other's throats, either in the courts or through public slanging matches in the media.

The last court case between the couple in 2011 had resulted in Katie being made to pay Peter an undisclosed sum and publicly apologise after claims he cheated on her and that he didn't love Harvey.

Court cases aside and behind closed doors there was further evidence of strained relations between the two concerning Katie's eldest son, Harvey. Peter's access to the disabled tot, which soon after their divorce had been every other weekend, continued to be a sticking point. While Katie herself admitted Peter was very much the primary father figure in Harvey's life, seeing him regularly was still proving something of a problem.

'I saw him yesterday at his school. It was like a dream seeing my boy,' Peter told *Now* magazine in September 2012. 'He wouldn't leave me alone. It was all Daddy this, Daddy that. He drew me a beautiful picture. The kid's really incredible.

'There are a few little complications at the moment about my seeing him. That's something I can't really talk about. But I have every faith that we'll get it sorted. It's happened before. Harvey's going to be in my life forever.'

But after a period of relative calm over the Christmas period as Peter tried to come to terms with Andrew's death, the pair were embroiled in yet another explosive fall-out after Katie's shock wedding to a part-time stripper. The first her former husband knew of the Bahamas ceremony was seeing pictures of the beachside nuptials on the internet while he was at home looking after their two children, Junior, now seven and five-year-old Princess.

Having dated bodybuilding Kieran for just six weeks and with family members knowing very little about her new spouse, Peter's immediate concern was the impact another husband would have on the vulnerable youngsters' lives and what they were learning about marriage.

For him there was a sense of déjà vu about the whole affair too. Katie's second marriage to Alex Reid, three years previously, had been another top secret affair, which again Peter had only found out about following a phone call some hours after the Las Vegas ceremony had taken place. At least, one could argue, Katie had dated Alex for a good six months before making the commitment and therefore Peter knew something of his children's new stepfather.

Twenty-five-year-old Kieran had been on the scene for just two months and while he seemed pleasant enough, the little that was publicly known about him was unlikely to have been music to Peter's ears. Aside from his day job as a plasterer, Kieran had made several appearances as a stripper on TV, including a stint on BBC soap *EastEnders*, while his half-naked images regularly appeared on gay websites. He had also reportedly stripped naked for a gay fan on a webcam.

But calling him 'a true gentleman', Katie started dating her new lover just a few weeks after splitting from Argentinian model Leandro Penna.

Introduced through friend Phil Turner, her make-up artist Gary Cockerill's husband, it was obvious Katie's new relationship was moving at break-neck speed – even rivalling her fast-moving romance with Peter, which saw the couple getting engaged just three months after meeting in the TV jungle.

'From the moment I told Leo to leave last year, I wanted to stay single and I said I was going to. But obviously that didn't last long!

'That's because I've been swept off my feet – it's a similar feeling to when I met Pete,' Katie explained to the *Sun*.

But whereas Peter resisted Katie's pleas to get engaged within 24 hours of officially becoming an item, her new husband-to-be proposed three weeks into dating, when he got down on one knee on Christmas Day.

The engagement had been shock news in itself, but few believed it would actually lead to marriage less than a month later. Even her mum Amy, who had been close to Pete during his marriage to Katie, expressed concern that the fledgling couple had moved too quickly.

Peter, meanwhile, had 'no idea what to tell the children'.

While Katie had told the youngsters something of what was going on, there was still some explaining to do in preparation for her return to the UK, complete with husband and new stepfather.

'Junior and Princess were staying with their dad when Jordan and Kieran tied the knot and she spoke to them about the wedding in a roundabout way before she went, but will tell them, with presents, when she's back,' a friend divulged.

'Pete's worried Princess thinks getting married is an everyday thing,' a close pal of Peter's explained further to *Closer* magazine. 'He's told the kids it's a special commitment to a person you love and want to spend the rest of your life with.

'He doesn't give a toss about her marrying again, but he can't believe she'd do this to the kids, they'd only just got used to Leo.'

With Peter's 'furious' reaction splashed across the press, Katie hit back, saying she didn't want to get drawn into an argument with her former husband over their children and slammed 'people surrounding her ex' for getting involved. She also dismissed claims that Junior and Princess hadn't been told about her wedding, while Pete's agents reiterated the point that he had not publicly spoken to any family or friends about the nuptials.

In a lengthy statement on her website, Katie wrote: 'I know my marriage to Kieran is going to attract criticism and that there will be people selling stories on the back of their perception of me and my decision.

'I will take that criticism on the chin and argue my corner where I feel it is necessary.

'What I won't do is get dragged into a tit-for-tat

argument with Pete about the children to be played out in public – they are old enough to read these things.

'I know he [Peter] has people around him that would want him to do an article running me down if I took up stamp collecting, let alone get married quickly but I believe him to be a bigger man than that.

'If Pete has an issue or concerns, he has my number. Pete is a good father – everyone knows he loves our children. So do I.

'Our children are happy and healthy, as he knows. I discussed with them at length what I was doing and why. I wish Pete nothing but love and luck with his relationship with Emily, who seems delightful.'

Although the statement showed all her usual fighting spirit, Katie was clearly trying to hold an olive branch out to Peter. A month later, with more shock news that she had fallen pregnant on her honeymoon, the singer was set to be approached by her third husband, who wanted to smooth things over.

'Kieran really cares about her kids and wants to get off on the right foot because his child will be a half-brother or half-sister to Peter's two children,' a friend claimed. 'He's making sure his child, Princess and Junior all have the right upbringing and he wants a relationship with their father.'

Kieran himself admitted he was enjoying getting to know Peter's children and felt lucky to be part of their lives.

'I can't wait to see Kate bloom throughout the pregnancy but most of all, I'm excited at the prospect of settling down with her and bringing up a family,' Kieran said about impending fatherhood. 'I fell head over heels in love with Kate and that feeling hasn't changed. The more I get to know her and her kids, the more I feel honoured to be part of the family.'

Whether a meeting would ever take place between Peter and Kieran remained to be seen but the trio's relationship had hardly set off on the best foot. Not only had Peter not been told about the wedding, he had reportedly learned about Katie's baby news after reading about it in a newspaper.

The former Page 3 girl had chosen to announce it on the front page of the *Sun* newspaper, where she had a weekly column and admitted while it hadn't been planned, she was over the moon at having a fourth child.

Peter remained tight-lipped on the subject but there was no doubt it heralded a new and potentially difficult era for him. While it was happy news that his children would have a new sibling, there was no getting away from the fact that once again he would have to cope with a new man making a very public attempt at being a father figure to them.

As Peter was approaching his 40th birthday, which by all accounts should have been a time of celebration, the singer was left 'heartbroken and fuming' when a picture appeared on the internet of Kieran cooking with a grinning Junior and Princess by his side. The photo, believed to have been taken by Katie, was uploaded onto Twitter with the caption: 'Pancakes with the family!!!!!!!!'

To an outsider, it could quite conceivably be father, son and daughter enjoying some quality time at home together – and it was alarmingly similar to the first snaps of Katie's second husband Alex playing with Peter's kids in the park, which had triggered one of his worst ever panic attacks.

While Peter had come a long way since then, there was no denying that seeing his family with another man came at a very difficult time when he was still grieving the loss of his brother.

But on the eve of his birthday, Katie still appeared determined to make peace with Peter and was one of the first to wish him a 'happy birthday'. In a cryptic message on her Twitter profile just before midnight she tapped out: 'Happy birthday an [sic] have a fabulous day and year x.'

Even though her legal case against Peter continued to ramble on, Katie's pregnancy was making her review her consistently strained relationship with her former husband.

'I want to make peace with Pete, life's too short – I'm done with fighting,' she told a friend.

True, she had been married twice since their split, but now well into the pregnancy with her first baby since having children with Peter, it was reminding her of the happy days they had once shared together. Not only that, when her son Harvey was taken to hospital soon after her baby announcement, Peter's absence at his bedside was poignant.

'Being in hospital with Harvey reminded her of how she and Pete used to support each other and she's contacted him to let him know how Harvey's doing.

'She said it would have been great if he could've visited Harvey in hospital and that she wished things could be "good between us for the sake of building our extended family". This pregnancy has definitely changed her. She's almost seemed vulnerable over the last couple of weeks –

she's very reflective and emotional. She just wants peace with Pete,' a friend revealed.

Writing about the ordeal in a message to her 1.7 million fans on her Twitter page, Katie said: 'Held my little boy's hand while he was being put to sleep boo hooooo.' When a fan asked if Peter had visited the tot, she replied: 'Nope x.'

While Peter publicly remained silent on the incident, a friend confirmed that he would have loved to visit Harvey in hospital but was looking after Princess and Junior at the time.

'He had the kids last week, so wasn't able to. But he's hoping he can spend time with him soon,' the source added.

And while Peter may have been struggling to get his head around Katie's latest set-up with new husband and child, he had maintained long ago that he wanted to distance himself from her life, aside from mutual care of the children.

And now more than ever, Peter had plenty going on in his own world to fill his valuable time and headspace.

Still grieving the loss of Andrew, the singer plunged himself back into work in a bid to move on from the toughest year of his life. Back on the road again, he finished off his rescheduled *Up Close And Personal* tour and determined to keep his spirits up, filming of the new series of his ITV2 show, *Peter Andre: My Life*, followed hot on its heels.

'The first night back on tour in Cambridge went well, and it was good to be back. I'm happy to be working again because it gives me something to focus on, which has really helped.

'It's when I stop that I find it difficult, and it's going to be a long time before things feel normal again,' he admitted in his column.

It wasn't just business as usual for Peter, though. Emily had returned to Bristol University after the Christmas holidays and after all they had been through over the festive period, the singer was missing his girlfriend more than ever.

'Emily is back at uni and working very hard, so we haven't been seeing as much of each other – especially as I'm also on tour. Right now, I'm probably missing her even more than usual because of everything that's happened, but it's good in a way because she's doing her job and I'm doing mine.

'Although we've known each other for two and a half years, January 16 was actually our six-month anniversary of being together. We celebrated quietly and privately – that's as much as I'll say!'

Although he was clearly feeling the distance between them, Emily remained devoted to the singer and was supporting him in whatever way she could. On the night of the 2013 National Television Awards in London, Peter's first public outing since Andrew's death, critics praised the 'hot couple' for co-ordinating in black as they made their entrance on the red carpet.

Feeling upbeat, Peter said afterwards: 'Emily and I had an amazing night at the NTAs, and didn't she look beautiful? We poked our heads into the after-party, but it was so rammed, that's all we could get in! Now Emily's finished her uni exams, it's been brilliant to spend some time with her. I was meant to be going to Australia in February, but for various reasons, I'm not going there anymore. One of the main reasons is that I want to be here for Valentine's Day.'

Finally, he had found a relationship since his marriage to Katie that was moving very much in the right direction. However, the pair hadn't been immune to rumours, which had provided endless conflicting stories in the press, including a secret marriage, a number of break-ups, plans to move in with each other and one or both of them having cold feet. But the truth was a lot more clean-cut.

'She's made a big impact on my life and I know I always say it's early days, but it is,' Peter explained. 'In this industry there seems to be an expectation that things happen quickly but we've taken our time and everything as it is right now is great.

'The funny thing is about three months ago stories came out saying she had cold feet and three months later we're still together. All we can do is show it with time but there are no issues.'

Their future together looked promising and while mutual desire for each other showed no sign of waning, there was one whisper which simply wouldn't go away: the 16-year age gap meant compromises would have to be made.

While Peter was desperate to extend his family, trainee doctor Emily had four years to go before finishing her studies, which some in his close circle claimed was weighing heavily on his mind. After graduating in June 2014, Emily was set to follow a two-year foundation programme and placement in a hospital, meaning Peter would be nearing 45 before he could even contemplate making his dream of having more children a reality.

'It's dawned on Pete that he'll have to wait a long time before the next chapter in his life begins,' a friend revealed.

'They've only been dating nine months but he's madly in love, she's everything to him. He knows she doesn't want kids for years because she's too young and wants to concentrate on university and career. He wants to move the relationship forward but it'll be a while before she can do that.'

Publicly, Peter also hinted he'd put his dreams of a larger family on hold, saying, 'I definitely, definitely want more kids in the future but I'm still a spring chicken, really.' But for the time being at least, he had more control over his life than ever before and as he turned 40, the singer had achieved more than he'd ever thought possible.

He had a music career spanning 20 years, a glittering TV career, three beautiful children and a devoted girlfriend he wanted to spend the rest of his life with. Even his ex-wife looked set to bury the hatchet once and for all. And with all that under his belt, reaching the landmark age signalled a new lease of life for him as well.

'I feel I'm turning 30, I don't think I look 40. Age is just a number. If you are 80 and rocking it in nightclubs, you might have to think twice but turning 40 to me is nothing,' he insisted.

But while he had much to celebrate, he definitely wasn't

in the mood for the huge blowout in Las Vegas he'd dreamed of a year previously.

The one thing he did want was the one thing he couldn't have.

'The only thing I would really like is to have my brother Andrew back with me,' he said, 'but obviously that's one birthday wish that isn't going to come true, sadly.'

So in difficult circumstances Pete decided to keep the day low-key. After spending the morning riding Formula One simulators with his brothers, followed by a spot of shopping with his children, the millionaire singer topped the day off with a lavish champagne meal with Emily and a group of friends at a top London restaurant.

It hadn't been quite the massive party he'd once envisaged but with a trip to America with Emily planned for later in the year, the ever down-to-earth Peter knew that what really mattered was he had reached 40 with plenty to be grateful for.

'Obviously there was someone missing from my birthday and I found that tough,' he explained. 'Although it's been hard, I do realise how lucky I am to have brilliant children, the most loyal friends, the best management and an amazingly beautiful girlfriend.'

And even more importantly, the show didn't stop there... the future was looking just as bright.

At the start of his music career Peter had dreamed of playing to 12,000 fans at Wembley Arena. Having ticked that ambition off the list several times, he now had his eyes fixed on playing the 90,000-capacity Wembley Stadium before giving up singing for good.

'I'll do Wembley Stadium one day. I think I can do it in the next two years and then I'll hang my hat up,' he revealed.

As well as a new reggae track recorded with old friend and rapper Shaggy, Peter's TV career was also going from strength to strength. After picking up a TRIC Award for Best Satellite/Digital TV Personality for the second year running, just weeks after his 40th, he admitted to being in secret talks with ITV about moving away from reality shows and into an exciting, new project on the small screen.

'I've just been given a great new format show for ITV,' he revealed after the show. 'I'm slowly moving into a lot more format so that in the next two years, or maybe even in the next year, there'll be less reality.'

Never one to rest on his laurels and ever following his businessman dad's words of wisdom on investing his hard-earned cash outside the showbiz industry, Peter was also in talks to open a third coffee shop. Staying true to the Andrea tradition of keeping it in the family, the singer had big ideas of expanding his New York Coffee Club brand, which also meant laying down a foundation for his children to follow in his footsteps.

'We've already got two five-star cafes in East Grinstead and Brighton but we might be opening one in London. We've always wanted to keep expanding the business and are hoping to open ten in the UK before moving to New York to open a big one there,' he announced. 'It's all very exciting and I love the idea that the kids could take over the business one day.'

Peter's now global status was also bringing with it some rather more bizarre additions to his CV, including being made a surprise ambassador of Malta's capital city Valletta. After being unanimously voted by city councillors to promote the rich history and art of the world heritage site, furious locals signed a petition to get him sacked but Peter was happy and honoured to do the job.

Aside from winning Best International Male at the Malta Music Awards the week previously, Peter had no link with the island but promised to promote the holiday destination on his ITV2 show.

It was a bizarre role indeed but then again, his career seemed ever-evolving and there were no hard and fast rules as to which direction it would take next. Long gone were the days when his sole ambition was to be a Michael Jackson impersonating pop star with a distant dream of 'making it big' in England. Over the past 40 years he had gone from bullied schoolboy to cheesy pin-up, to reality TV star, credible music artist, fashion designer, charity ambassador, faithful husband and devoted father.

There had been the most incredible highs and the most devastating lows but whatever had come his way, he had got through each day in the only way he knew how – with a brave face, the classic Andre smile and a determination to put on a damn good show, both on and off stage. And there was no doubt about it, his close-knit family could take credit for keeping the superstar on the straight and narrow. They were the constant in his life that had kept him focused in sometimes very tough circumstances.

His parents, Savva and Thea, continued to be an inspiration and Peter was thankful for their almost 60 years of marriage and strong religious beliefs for grounding him so early in life, something that had stood him in such good stead through adulthood. Even after his divorce from Katie, he still wanted to follow in their footsteps and try again at recreating the secure family unit he'd grown up in.

And in the most testing time of all, in the wake of losing their beloved brother Andrew, his siblings continued to bolster each other in a tremendous show of unity and strength.

'Regarding losing a loved one; 'You don't get over it, you get on with it' Wise words bruvs @mrmichaelandre,' Peter wrote on Twitter in a touching message to his brother Michael, who was still one of his greatest counsellors.

And his emotional and physical safety net had now expanded further with Emily now on the scene. Having credited the MacDonagh family with saving him from plummeting into a very dark place during his brother's cancer battle, they had also been on hand to help him and his children through some of his toughest life events to date.

'Emily's been there and her whole family have been a support. My kidney stones operation, getting my brother into the Royal Marsden hospital – that was all down to them. I owe a lot to them. My kids absolutely love Emily and her whole family.'

Turning 40 clearly marked a new and exciting chapter for Peter and with reaching the milestone had come some all-important wisdom. Armed with more experiences in four decades than most people could expect in just one lifetime yet still happy with his lot, the singer-turned-TV star finally knew who the real Peter Andre was.

'I know my bad points. Yes, I'm vain; yes, I can be ridiculous at times, but I know who I am and I know the importance of humility, the importance of not believing the hype and getting carried away with your own ego.

'At the end of the day people can just decide they don't want you around anymore and then it's all over. That day will come to all of us – you're an idiot to think it won't. For now, I'm just trying to make the most of what I have.'

And that's what makes Peter Andre the star he is today – always trying to do the best he can and never, ever taking life too seriously. Because after all, life's just too short, and he knows that more than anybody now.